Contents

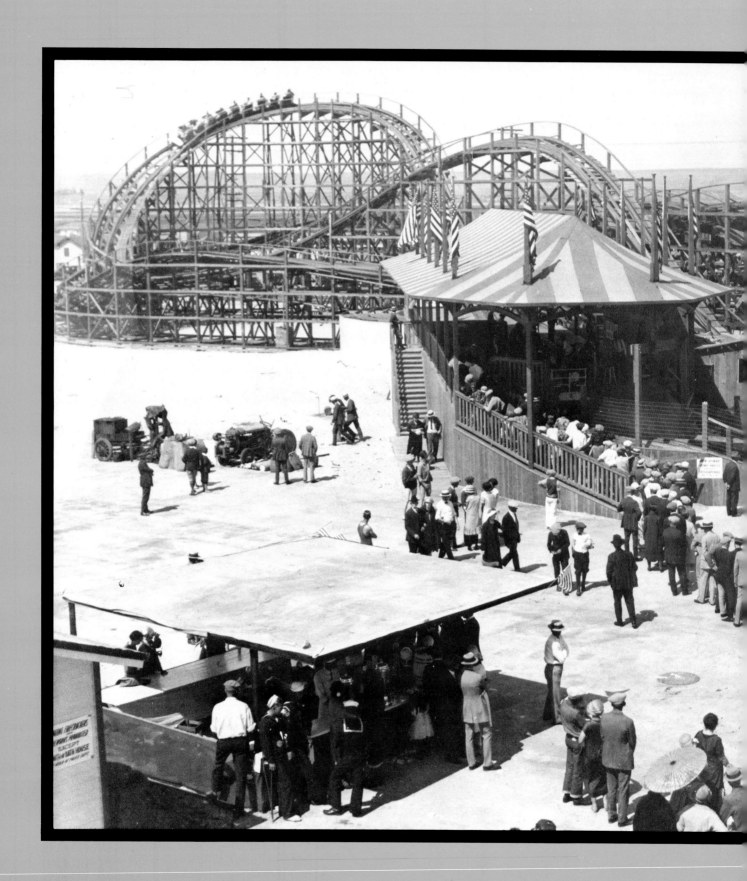

Introduction

In recent years San Diegans have taken to calling their city "America's Finest." Considering the lovely site, superb climate, impressive institutions, recreational and cultural opportunities, it is a plausable designation. San Diego, however, was not always a candidate for the title "America's Finest City." In its infancy, it was a dirty, isolated and desolate place. It was called by various visitors the "last corner of the earth," and "a quiet even dead and desolated place." Another called San Diego "a little mud town" with neither "an imposing or interesting appearance." The same writer referred to San Diego's most persistent and most commented on early residents, the fleas: "Go where you will you will be infested with them;" indeed he said that at that very moment "the little rascals keep my flesh crawling & so torment me that I can scarcely write." Even as late as 1916, when Donal Hord (future sculptor of distinction) arrived by boat, he was so shocked by the barren, brown setting that he cried.

San Diego: A Pictorial History illustrates the transformation of San Diego from a desolate little village on the last corner of the earth to the seventh largest city in the nation, with the proud—if self-proclaimed—distinction of being one of the most livable places in the United States. The book focuses on the people (of many races and cultures) who did it, the institutions, and the setting. It traces the emergence of the basic infrastructure—water, railroads, streets and highways, the harbor, aviation, commerce, and the military. It covers the booms and busts, some of the good and some of the bad. San Diego: A Pictorial History also documents the creation of a strong sense of identity, especially through the use of Hispanic architecture and historic sites and the history and mythology of its pre-Anglo roots. The development of Balboa Park, the Zoo and the Wild Animal Park, Mission Bay Park, and the Embarcadero (the waterfront) are likewise traced. The book will also show the major economic factors which have shaped the city's development. Although this volume covers from first Spanish notice of the area to the present, the major focus is on the last century during which San Diego emerged from a sleepy village into a major American city.

THE SAN DIEGO EXPOSITION

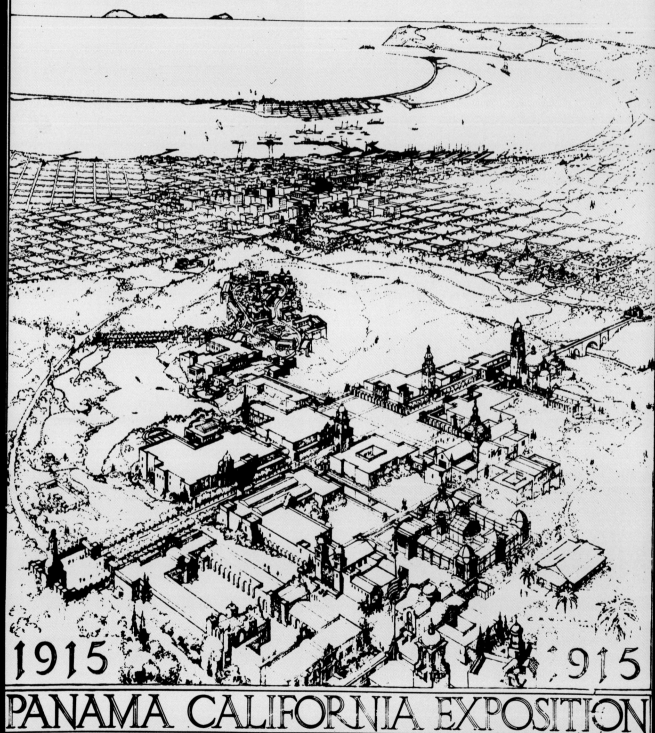

1915   915

PANAMA CALIFORNIA EXPOSITION

Acknowledgments

Many people make possible a book like this. The sources of much of the historical information are acknowledged in the bibliography. Many other individuals helped in many other ways. It is impossible to mention each and every one, although their individual contributions are known and appreciated by the author. It is only possible to list those whose help extended beyond the ordinary: Jerry Hebert, who provided unique photographs which have never been published before; Mame De Pew, who gave me free run of the San Diego High School Alumni Association's records; the late Howard Gardner of the Klauber Wangenheim Company, Anna MacPherson of the Save our Heritage Organization, Donna Damson and Georgeanne Irving at the San Diego Zoo; Brenda Hughes at the San Diego Opera; William Eaton of the Old Globe; Beverly Schroeder of the Center City Development Corporation, Ed Navarro of Old Town State Park; Elizabeth Arbizo of the University of California San Diego Public Information Office; Be Barnes of the San Diego Padres; Alan Thewlis of the San Diego Maritime Museum; Linda Fiske at The Museum of Man; Rhoda Kruse at the San Diego Public Library; Lyn Olsson and Stephen Colston of the San Diego State University Center for Regional History, and Ruth Leerhoff of their Special Collections; Ronald and Dale Ballou May, who provided photographs and much other assistance; and Ray T. Smith, who helped with Vietnamese materials.

The contribution of Ken Jacques, who handled with skill and enthusiasm much of the photocopying and some photographing for the book, was of immense value. Indeed, his work really entitles him to a place on the title page as my technical advisor on the book. Alexandra Luberski helped in many ways, including the critiquing of chapters within her specialty.

At San Diego State University, Dean Robert Detweiler of the College of Arts and Letters provided funds for typing, and also provided much encouragement. The staff of the History Department helped in many ways.

The staffs of many repositories were very helpful, but few so much so as the San Diego Historical Society. Special thanks are due to Gregg Hennessey, Bruce Kamerling, Howard Welty, Cynthia Richert, Stephen Wolz, and especially to Larry Booth and Jane Booth.

The person to whom the major debt is owed, however, is Sylvia Arden. She has given generously of her time and expertise in getting me into this project, in helping with the research, in reading texts and captions, and in offering continual encouragement. For her help on this book, her help in introducing me to San Diego history, and on behalf of all local historians of San Diego for her superb role in protecting and caring for the largest collection of materials on San Diego history, this book is respectfully dedicated to Sylvia Arden.

Raymond Starr
San Diego State University

The name *California* came from a fifteenth century romantic Spanish novel, *Las sergas de Esplandian* (The Exploits of Explandian) by Garcia Ordonez de Montalvo. The novel was set in a mystical island ruled by an Amazon queen Calafia. The description and the exploits of its inhabitants seized the imagination of the Spaniards of the day. Since they thought the peninsula we call Baja California was an island, the name *California* got attached to it—by whom and just when, we do not know. Even though the Spanish knew by 1539 the area was not an island, the concept—and the name—remained for a very long time—witness this 1776 German map from John Oldmixon, *Des Britische in America* (1776). Thus, from the very beginning, there has been a mystical quality attached to the name which has helped to convey the image of California—and as a part of it, San Diego as a special place. Map courtesy of the San Diego State University Special Collections.

The Hispanic Period 1542-1846

Since June 1542 the Spanish vessel *San Salvador*, commanded by Juan Rodriquez Cabrillo, had been working its way up the west coast of North America. On Thursday, September 28, the explorers "found a very good enclosed port, to which they gave the name of San Miguel." The expedition stayed in the area for several days of fishing, exploring and establishing less-than-friendly relations with the native population; and then continued northward.

Cabrillo and his crew were probably the first Europeans to visit the site of present-day San Diego. The place they saw was a promising one. It included one of the finest natural harbors on the eastern rim of the Pacific Ocean, a sizable body of water separated from the vicissitudes of the ocean by a large sandbar island, with a protected entry under the lee of a large peninsula, later called Point

Loma. There was a river draining into the bay with a fair amount of level land around the bay and in the river valley. To the east was a chain of mountains which provided a natural barrier protecting the area from a harsh desert. This gave the region a mild summer climate and a balmy winter. Unfortunately, the area was also quite arid, with less than ten inches of rain a year. Indeed, the little area duplicated to an astounding degree the climates of the Mediterranean countries, which many consider to be the finest in the world. Although the mountains would make future land transportation difficult and probably would keep the area from becoming a major industrial-commercial center, the pleasantness of the setting and the mildness of the climate would be the foundation for subtropical agriculture, for tourism, and for people seeking a quality life. It is doubtful Cabrillo and his men knew it, but they had come across a special corner of the earth.

The Spaniards did little to follow up Cabrillo's findings; they did not visit this "special corner" again until 1602 when Sebastian Vizcaino led three ships into the harbor. Vizcaino and his men also spent several days in the area, holding the first Roman Catholic services on California soil, and renaming the bay *San Diego* after a priest from the Spanish town of Alcala who had been canonized for his piety, poverty, and medical work.

For the next 150 years the Spanish continued to ignore the renamed bay. It was not until the 1760s, when the Spanish began to fear the incursions of the English, French, and Russians, that they took steps to settle San Diego Bay and other sites in what was being called *Alta California*. In 1769 the Spanish dispatched naval and overland expeditions to San Diego Bay in order to establish a *presidio* (fortified settlement) and a mission. At first the sailors camped by the bay, but when the rest of the party arrived (including the priest, Junipero Serra) they established a wooden palisade and a crude chapel on the side of a hill near the mouth of the San Diego River. When Father Serra blessed the mission and the fort on July 16, 1769, it could be said that San Diego was founded.

Although others were on the site earlier, the figure most San Diegans associate with the founding of their city is Father Serra. As part of the plan to colonize Alta California, Serra and his group came to San Diego, where they established the mission, San Diego de Alcala, in 1769. Serra then moved on northward to found other missions in a chain which finally reached twenty-one and ranged from San Diego to north of San Francisco. The mission he founded in San Diego was designed to bring Christianity to the native Indians, to introduce them to "civilized" ways, and to establish the core of a Spanish community. It was a moderately successful mission, with nearly two thousand Indian residents at its peak.

The Indians to be Christianized were descendents of those who had exchanged blows with Cabrillo's men in 1542. They were of the Yuman linguistic group, and the Spanish usually called them *Diguenos*. Recently, however, both Native Americans and scholars have begun to use the word *Kumeyaay* to refer to all of the Indians of the Yuman linguistic group who live in the San Diego coastal, mountainous, and desert areas. These Indians lived a relatively simple life, utilizing the gentle environment in a sensible way. They ate acorns, hunted small animals, and gathered seafood from the coastline, including whales which washed ashore. Their dwellings were simple brush structures and their tools were usually wood, stone, or shell. The local Indians wore scarcely any clothes, as few were needed. Politically, they were not highly

The commander of the first European expedition to see San Diego is a mystery man. We do not know what he really looked like. We are not even sure whether he was Spanish (Juan Rodriquez Cabrillo) or Portuguese (Joao Rodriques Cabrilho). We do know he served Spain and was appointed leader of the expedition which sailed out of Navidad on June 27, 1542, to explore the northern coast of New Spain. After passing through what would become San Diego, his expedition went north where Cabrillo was wounded and died on January 3, 1543. This photograph by Marco Thorne is of a statue of Cabrillo (about which more will be said later) which is currently located at the Cabrillo National Monument on Point Loma. Photograph courtesy of the San Diego Historical Society Public Library Collection

organized, with extended family groups probably the essence of their political structure. The Kumeyaay's religious beliefs stressed symbols and rituals relating to nature. There was nothing in their world—secular or religious—which would make them especially good candidates for missionizing.

Although the prospects cannot have been very good, the Spanish did try hard to make their mission work. When it became obvious the Presidio Hill location was not going to succeed, Father Serra obtained permission to move the mission several miles up the San Diego River to its current site. After surviving an Indian uprising and the killing of one of the priests, the missionaries built a church plus shops, residences, and work buildings. They developed vineyards, orchards, cultivated fields, and raised cattle. To provide water the fathers built a dam and irrigation system utilizing the San Diego River. In time, they also built a sub-mission at Santa Ysabel, in the Backcountry.

Within the mission system, the lives of the Indians were tightly regulated. They were instructed in Christianity, taught crafts and skills, and worked hard in the mission, the fields, or wherever else they were needed. The unmarried Indians were segregated by sex and they were flogged or put in stocks for many offenses. It was a harsh system (indeed, it was flogging which probably touched off the 1774 Indian revolt) although apologetic scholars point out the harshness was no worse than that practiced in Europe at the time. In recent years historians have tended to criticize the mission system severely, stressing the high death rate, the deprivation of freedom, and calling it disguised slavery or a version of a concentration camp.

The mission was only part of San Diego during the short Spanish era, 1769 to 1822. There was also the

The voyage which resulted in the European discovery of San Diego Bay was part of a larger Spanish program of exploration in the Pacific region. It was designed to discover the mythical "Northwest Passage" and to prevent England or France from getting a foothold in the area. The particular voyage which Cabrillo commanded began at Navidad on the west coast of Mexico on June 27, 1542, and consisted of two ships, the larger *San Salvador* and the smaller *Victoria*.

As for the actual discovery of San Diego Bay, we know little. The official and full log of the expedition has not been found; we only have a later, abridged version. About all we know of the event is contained in that account, which is quoted in full in a translation by James Robert Moriarty III and Mary Keistman:

> On Thursday [September 28, 1542] they went about six leagues north-northwest along the coast and found a very good enclosed port, to which they gave the name of San Miquel. It lies at 34 degrees 20 minutes, and after anchoring they went ashore, where there were people. Of these, three waited, and all the others ran away. To these three they gave some gifts, and the Indians told them by signs that people like the Spaniards had passed inland; they showed with much fear. At night the Spaniards

left the ships in a small boat to land and to fish. There happened to be Indians there, and they began to shoot with their arrows and they wounded three men.

> The next day in the morning they went with the boat further into the port, which was large, and caught two boys who understood nothing, not even signs, and they gave them shirts and soon sent them away. . . . While in port, a very large storm passed, but because the port was so good they felt nothing. The weather came from the west-southwest, and south southwest, and it was rainy. This was the first real storm they had undergone, and they stayed in the port until the following Tuesday. Here the natives called the Christians "Guacamal."

> On Tuesday, the 3rd of October, they left the port of San Miquel, . . .

We have no contemporary sketches of Cabrillo's visit. The three illustrations here are reproductions of paintings done by Robert F. Geise for the Cabrillo National Monument. The first painting shows the two ships at full sail. The second is how Geise imagines the first landing took place, and the third depicts the shirt incident described in the account quoted above. Photographs courtesy of the Cabrillo National Monument

presidio, where virtually all San Diegans not at the mission lived, although that population probably never exceeded four hundred to five hundred whites at any time. San Diego started very slowly.

San Diego became a Mexican possession with the successful revolution of New Spain; the flag ceremony recognizing the change in sovereignty occurred in the presidio in 1822. In the Mexican era, several significant developments occurred: the secularization of the mission, the ranchero system, the growth of the town outside the presidio walls, and the granting of *pueblo* (town) status.

The establishment of the town outside the fortress walls was certainly the most significant change. By the early 1820s life inside the presidio had become so deplorable that the commander allowed some retired and disabled soldiers to build houses outside the fort walls; by 1830 there were perhaps ten or twelve dwellings built around a plaza. In time some substantial adobe buildings were erected, and that was San Diego until the 1870s and Alonzo Horton's successful efforts to move it closer to the water.

The first political organization of San Diego came after the town spilled out of the presidio. In 1835 San Diego was granted pueblo status, with the accompanying grant of land and political power. Since the population soon dwindled to about 150, the Mexican government rescinded pueblo status, apparently without any local protest. Despite this, the little town was active in the confused political world of the Mexican period. There were severe conflicts between California and the central government; there were also conflicts within California between north and south. Amidst the confusion, several armed revolts occurred. During one, San Diego became the seat of government for California; during another, San Diego citizen Pio Pico secured control over the province and became *de facto* governor of California.

Part of the Mexican rule included the secularization of the mission system. In the 1830s, the mission chapels became parish churches, and the land and livestock was disposed of in various ways. For the most part, the mission Indians were left dispersed, and dispossessed; the *Californios* (inhabitants of Hispanic California) acquired large grants of former mission land in the *rancho* system. In that system the Mexican government made large land grants to people. In San Diego County, thirty-two grants were made, ranging from 2 acres to 133,441 acres in size. Three went to Indians; two to military men for meritorious service; and the rest to whomever had the political connections. The effect was to destroy the mission system and impoverish the Indians, and to impede the growth of the town, as much of the population became dispersed over the countryside in the ranchos. Californio ranchos raised cattle in sizable numbers to serve the hide and tallow trade, and some provided beef to the goldminers after 1849. After the American takeover most Mexican landowners lost control of their ranchos, usually to enterprising Americans. The ranches themselves lasted a long time; indeed some are still in existence.

The ruins of the missions and ranchos have inspired the myth of a romantic California. The myth gained strength in the 1880s when the real estate developers encouraged it for the benefit of tourism, and was further enhanced by the Hollywood film makers. The Arcadian legend depicted an era of *dons* (Spanish gentlemen) living in pastoral paradise as feudal lords on giant estates. The dons were supposed to be "devoted to the grand and primary business of the enjoyment of life" in a pastoral, patriarchial "almost Arcadian existence." Recent historians have challenged this concept, and shown that life in the Hispanic period was nothing like that depicted in the legends. In San Diego in particular, the political turmoil, Indian hostilities, local strife, and transportation problems all worked together to prevent the growth of opulence and a lavish life style, although a few citizens did find prosperity.

This, then, was the Mexican San Diego which the Americans seized in 1846. San Diego was described by visitors as a small dirty town below an abandoned presidio with a population of only several hundred. That being the case, what is the importance of the Spanish-Mexican period of San Diego's history? In some ways, not very much. Most of the people who provided the impetus for the move to a better location, and to the development and promotion of San Diego, came after the American takeover. The political system is entirely American, although the pueblo land grant does stem from the Hispanic period. With some exceptions, most of the capital for development came from the new Americans. In the post-1870 period, most of the political and community leadership has been Anglo rather than Hispanic. Thus in many ways, San Diego is a modern American city with many characteristics shared by any other modern American city of similar size.

In other ways, however, the Hispanic heritage has been important. The Spanish did establish the settlement and make it work. The rancho system the Mexicans established was the basis of both later ranches and of many of the towns of San Diego County and the ranch agriculture continued to be important until the twentieth century. *Vaqueros* (Spanish and Indian cowboys) tended most ranches throughout San Diego history. Other Hispanics participated in the growth of the "New San Diego" and many intermarried with newly arrived Americans to bind together the old and new in the town.

The most important contribution of the Hispanic era, however, is probably the flavor or atmosphere it has contributed to the community. Especially as picked up and perpetuated in later years, a Hispanic flavor in architecture, in place names, and the use of Hispanic historical sites as symbols, has given a unique character to San Diego, one which gives the city an identity unlike any other in the country.

In most people's mind, Father Junipero Serra is the founding father of San Diego. He was born in Majorca and distinguished himself as a scholar before coming to Mexico in 1749 as a missionary. In 1767 he was made head of the missions in Baja California, and in 1769 established the San Diego mission. This was the first in a chain of missions (many founded by Serra) ranging from the San Diego Bay to north of San Francisco Bay. This chain was the effective starting point for the European settlement of California. By all accounts, Junipero Serra was an extraordinary man— compassionate toward the Indians, firm toward the military, and persistent in all things he considered important. Photograph courtesy of the San Diego Historical Society Research Archives

The mission did not prosper at its original site and was moved five miles up the San Diego River in 1774. Although there was a severe Indian attack just months after the move (which produced California's first Christian martyr, Father Luis Jayme); the mission was rededicated in 1777 and survived. A second church was dedicated in 1781, and the one we see in this picture was completed in 1813. The structure to the right of the church housed the priests; workshops, housing for Indians, and school rooms completed the quadrangle of the mission at its peak. There are no visual depictions of the mission prior to the Anglo-American period. This lithograph by Charles Koppel was done in 1853, after secularization and abandonment of the mission to the United States Army, which used it as a base for many years. Photograph from the author's collection

A mission served several purposes—to educate the Indians, to establish a self-sufficient economic and social unit, and to Christianize the Indians. For that purpose the Indians were brought to live at the mission. There at least some of each Indian's day was spent in religious instruction, as illustrated in this photograph of a model of the San Diego mission made by Edith Buckland Webb just before the Second World War. In the absence of contemporary visual records of the San Diego mission, the photographs of Webb's model are one of the best ways to visualize the operation of the Mission San Diego de Alcalá. Photograph courtesy of the Santa Barbara Mission Archive-Library

The missionaries wanted to "civilize" the Indians as well as Christianize them. Therefore, they tried to teach them crafts, agriculture and domestic arts. The women were trained in cooking, spinning and weaving cloth from the sheep raised on the mission, and sewing. They were also taught to do laundry and sometimes helped with cultivation of the crops. Often the wives of the soldiers stationed at the mission provided the instruction for the Indian girls and women. This photograph of the Webb model shows Indian women being taught kitchen skills. Photograph courtesy of the Santa Barbara Mission Archive-Library

While the women were taught "domestic arts," the men and boys at the San Diego mission were taught construction and agricultural skills. They ran an effective agricultural establishment, with vineyards, olive trees, cattle and sheep raising, and the cultivation of crops. The San Diego mission was, at its peak, the fourth most productive in California. At the same time, the Indians were taught how to make adobe bricks and tiles, and to construct and maintain western style buildings. This photograph of the Webb model shows the construction of a corridor, using poles as a base and tiles on top. This was a form of construction common to the time and place, and can be seen in many contemporary buildings in Old Town. Photograph courtesy of the Santa Barbara Mission Archive-Library

SANTA ISABEL.

In addition to the mission in the San Diego River valley, the Spanish also established other missionizing facilities in the area. In 1818 the San Diego mission built at Santa Ysabel an *assistencia* to serve as a chapel in the Backcountry. The Santa Ysabel chapel was designed to serve the needs of the large number of converts who lived in the area. It included, in addition to the chapel, outbuildings and corrals, as shown in a decayed condition in this 1853 drawing. Other mission establishments in the area included the large mission San Luis Rey Francia (1798) and its *assistencia* at Pala. Photograph courtesy of the San Diego Historical Society—Ticor Collection

Although glorified and romanticized by historians and in popular culture, the mission system in California—and San Diego—flourished for a very short period of time. In 1833 (only sixty-four years after San Diego de Alcala was founded) the Mexican government secularized the missions. The Indians were dispersed, much of the land was given to Californios as rancheros, and most of the mission buildings were converted to other use or simply crumbled into ruins. Mission San Diego went into a century-long decline, as illustrated in this Parker and Knight photograph from the late nineteenth century. Substantial restoration of the San Diego mission did not begin until the 1930s. Photograph courtesy of the California State Library

The Spanish *presidio* (fortified settlement) is, more than the mission, the point of origin for the founding of the town of San Diego. Constructed to provide accommodations for the military party, and protection for the mission, the presidio was dedicated the same time as the mission, July 16, 1769. The first presidio was a tule stockade, but in time it was replaced by earthworks and adobe buildings. Although anthropologist Paul Ezell stresses that the presidio was not the result of an official plan, it did develop into an establishment similar to most Spanish frontier forts. The presidio was built in a square, with a chapel and cemetery, barracks, officers' quarters, and other appropriate structures. There are no contemporary likenesses of the fort, but recently this 1820 map of the Presidio de San Diego was discovered in the Bancroft Library of the University of California. Photograph courtesy of The Bancroft Library, University of California, Berkeley

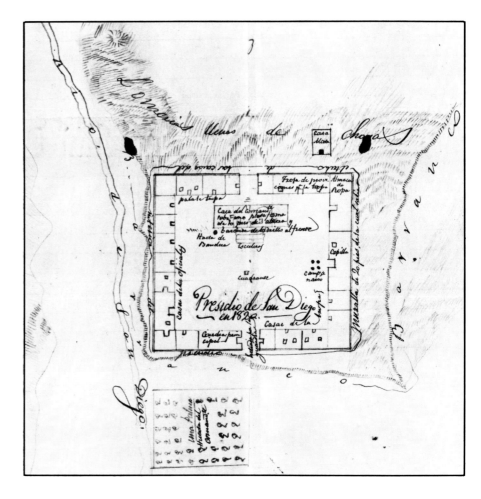

The presidio was gradually abandoned in the 1820s, as soldiers and their families began to move down the hill to the original site of San Diego (now called Old Town). On his first visit to San Diego in 1835, Richard Henry Dana described the presidio as being "in a most ruinous state." The ruins were spared total destruction in the early twentieth century when George Marston saw to their purchase and covered them with dirt. In 1965 the San Diego Historical Society began, under the leadership of San Diego State University professor Paul Ezell, the archaeological excavation of part of the ruins of the Spanish presidio. Much of what we know about the presidio and life in it is based on the analysis of artifacts from those excavations. The photograph shows some of the archaeologists digging in the chapel area. Note the observers behind the

security fence; the digging itself became a major tourist attraction. Photograph courtesy of the Center for Regional History, San Diego State University

One of the finds which generated much interest was a coffin lid with a large cross on it. This and other coffins enabled local historians to determine the burial site of a number of early residents. The excavations also told us much about the way the early residents lived. For instance, despite Spain's extremely restrictive trade policies, items found in the digs showed that the people of the area had a large number of goods from the Orient, eastern United States, and Europe. A catchment basin in which to collect water was discovered. There is evidence of typical Spanish ovens, which would indicate the introduction of wheat flour bread (which the Indians had not eaten). At the same time, persistence of barbecue pits and the nature of the animal bones showed that there were many native cooks in the presidio, as they cut meat and cooked it differently than the Europeans. Photograph courtesy of the Center for Regional History, San Diego State University

The other major Spanish structure on San Diego Bay, Fort Guijarros, was involved in the only naval "battle" fought at San Diego. Spanish policy forbade trade with other nations; Yankee merchants ignored that policy. The natural conflict inherent in this situation came to a head in 1803 when an American vessel, the *Lelia Byrd*, was caught engaging in trade with locals. Rather than surrender to the Spanish, the captain made a run for it. As she passed Fort Guijarros the Spanish fired, and *Lelia Byrd* fired back. Apparently neither side suffered much damage, and the ship fled safely. Another American ship, the *Franklin*, was fired on in 1828. Such efforts to prevent illegal trade seemed to have had little effect; between 1800 and 1828 at least thirty-one illegal merchant ships called at San Diego, mostly to obtain hides. This drawing by Gene Stout depicts Fort Guijarros and the exchange with the *Lelia Byrd*. Considering the ship's sails, one wonders about the wind conditions on that particular day! Photograph courtesy of the Fort Guijarros Museum Foundation

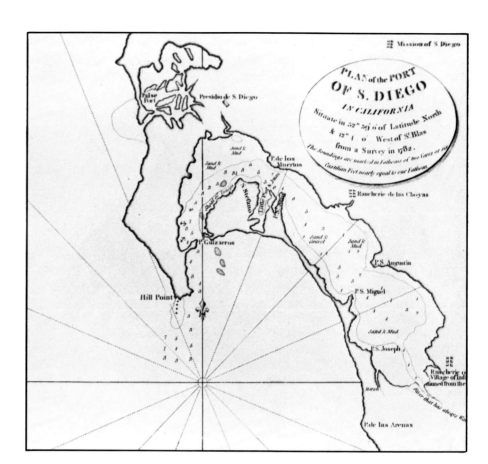

In the years between Cabrillo's exploration of the area and the end of the Spanish rule, a number of rough maps had been made of the San Diego region. The first really complete and accurate map was done after the survey by Juan Pantoja y Arriaga in 1782. It was published frequently in the years after 1782, including this 1798 edition by G. G. and J. Robinson of London. Map courtesy of the San Diego Historical Society Research Archives

San Diego was founded as a Spanish outpost; in 1822 it became a Mexican town. In that year the new Mexican government sent a commissioner to San Diego, who conducted a change of government ceremony in the plaza. A witness to the event has recorded that the officer ordered the troops to form in the plaza for the flagraising. There was, alas, no flag! Finally it was discovered that one soldier had a tiny Spanish flag on a little stick, and another had the new Mexican flag. The commandante then cried "Long Live the Mexican Empire!" and the tiny "Spanish flag was lowered and the Mexican flag raised in the midst of salvos of artillerymen and musketeers. After this the troops did nothing." The new flag they raised remained the Mexican flag until 1920, when it was changed somewhat. Drawing from Margaret Mackey and Louise P. Sooy, *Early California Costumes* (1932); courtesy of the Stanford University Press

The home illustrated in this photograph belonged to Juan Marron, at one time the *alcalde* (mayor) of San Diego. Note the exposed adobe construction on the end wall, and the barren hillside behind. Although this picture was taken much later, the presence of figures on horseback serves to remind us that in the Spanish-Mexican period, horseback, *carreta* (two-wheeled cart) or foot, were virtually the only means of transportation within San Diego. Photograph courtesy of The Bancroft Library, University of California, Berkeley

Throughout the Spanish period, the presidio *was* San Diego, as most inhabitants lived in it. Somewhere in the 1820s, Captain Francisco Maria Ruiz became the first to build a house outside the presidio. By the time of the American takeover in 1846 several hundred people lived in the small town, built in typical Hispanic fashion around a central plaza. While we have no photographs of the town during the Spanish and Mexican periods, the following pictures taken after the American takeover give a pretty accurate picture of what the town would have looked like.

The Machado y Silvas house was probably built in 1843, just before the Americans arrived. Of typical adobe construction, it faces the Plaza. Contrast the wood frame buildings to its right. They are Anglo-American and show how the Yankees brought their own wooden building styles with them. Photograph courtesy of The Bancroft Library, University of California, Berkeley

In the Mexican period (1822-1846), San Diego functioned as a fairly important outpost, playing a major part in the 1830 and 1844 uprisings. In the latter, San Diegan Pio Pico succeeded in taking control of the government, moving the capital to Los Angeles, and serving, for all practical purposes, as the last Mexican governor of California. Probably the most important result of the political disorder in the province was that it loosened ties with Mexico and made much easier the American takeover which occurred in 1846. This 1850 photograph shows Pio de Jesus Pico and his wife Maria Ygnacia Alvarado, whom he married in 1834. Photograph courtesy of the San Diego Historical Society—Ticor Collection

A major feature of the Mexican period of California history was the *rancho* system. Utilizing secularized mission and other land, Mexican officials made extensive land grants beginning in 1824. In San Diego County, thirty-two such grants were made. The ranches made important economic contributions to the area, especially in the production of hides and tallow. After the American conquest, many of the Californios lost their ranches, either because they could not prove ownership under the American legal system, or for economic reasons. Many of the ranches themselves survived for a long time as identifiable units; the Warner Rancho, illustrated here, is an example. While many continued to be producing ranches, others were the starting point for local towns. For example, National City was established on Rancho de la Nacion and Escondido developed on the El Rincon del Diablo Rancho. Brand and illustration from R. W. Brackett, *A History of the Ranchos* (1939)

The rancho and mission system of the Spanish-Mexican era gave rise in the late nineteenth century to the romantic California myth of an Arcadian system. The myth assumed that dashing dons spent their day riding silver-bejewelled horses about great estates while their senoras and senoritas, topped with mantillas, waited back in the hacienda. Periodically there were lavish balls and other entertainments. These woodcuts by Franz Geritz illustrate this myth.

As historian Charles Hughes has shown, the reality of Californio life on the ranches was a little less spectacular. Some Mexicans in California did acquire considerable wealth; in San Diego County Jose Antonio Aquirre, Juan Bandini, Jose Antonio Estudillo, Juan Marron, and Maria Pedrorena certainly did. But they did not live in an Arcadian paradise with the level of opulence depicted in the myth. Problems of transportation, political disorder, and Indian hostilities all worked to retard development, especially in the San Diego area, and to assure that the area remained relatively poor. Illustrations from Nellie Van de Grift Sanchez, *Spanish Arcadia* (1929)

Although one must be careful of the "Rancho Myth" in dealing with Hispanic San Diego, that does not mean that there were no substantial aspects to the ranchos and their contributions. One was the *vaquero*, or cowboy. Both Californios and Indians from the mission became vaqueros, and tended the herds of the missions and ranches in the Spanish-Mexican period. After the American takeover, Californio-Indian vaqueros continued to dominate the occupation until the twentieth century. Illustration from Jo Mora, *Californios* (1940)

Neophyte Mission Vaqueros

The missions and later the ranchos provided the foundation of San Diego's pre-American economy—the hide trade. They slaughtered huge herds of cattle, primarily for the horns, hides and tallow. The hides were dried and cured, then carted to hide houses on the bay where they were kept until ships—usually Yankee—arrived to purchase them. This hide trade began after 1822 but did not really take off until 1828; it remained significant for a generation. This Jo Mora drawing shows the hides being loaded into a carreta for the trip to a hide house. In showing Indian laborers and a Californio supervisor, it is probably a pretty accurate indication of the division of labor at that time. Illustration from Jo Mora, *Californios* (1940)

One of the sources of information about the hide houses in San Diego is the New Englander, Richard Henry Dana, Jr., whose *Two Years Before the Mast* (1840), described the San Diego hide trade: "For landing and taking on board hides, San Diego is decidedly the best place in California. The harbour is small and land-locked; there is no surf; the vessels lie within a cable's length of the beach; and the beach itself is smooth, hard sand, without rocks or stones.... The hides, as they come rough and un-cured from the vessels, are piled up outside the houses, whence they are taken and carried through a regular process of pickling, drying, cleaning, etc. and stowed away in the house, ready to be put on board." Photograph courtesy of the San Diego Historical Society—Ticor Collection

The first Anglo-Americans to come overland to San Diego were mountain men. Dressed in leather and living off the land, these frontiersmen penetrated the far west in the 1820s in search of furs and gold and adventure. Apparently the first to come to San Diego was the most famous, Jedediah Smith, who arrived in 1827. Sometime later Sylvester Pattie and his party came into town after traveling across Baja California. Inasmuch as the presence of foreigners was illegal by Mexican law, the mountain men were imprisoned and Sylvester Pattie died in prison at the presidio. It is not possible to say that the visits of the mountain men brought significant change to San Diego, although it is likely that their accounts of the place stimulated American interest in the area. Drawing from Margaret Mackey and Louise Sooy, *Early California Costumes* (1932); courtesy of the Stanford University Press

One of the first sketches of San Diego was done by the U.S. Army illustrator, John Mix Stanley, who made this drawing in 1846. It was reproduced as a lithograph in William H. Emory's *Notes of a Military Reconnaissance, From Fort Leavenworth, in Missouri to San Diego, California* (1848). Although the American presence is marked by the flag and the military tents to the left, the town was still basically the Mexican settlement, built around the central plaza with ranches on the outskirts. Photograph courtesy of The Bancroft Library, University of California, Berkeley

2

American Old Town 1846-1867

San Diego officially became an American town in 1846. As has often been the case, events well beyond San Diego Bay shaped its destiny. Since becoming free, Mexico had had trouble controlling her northern provinces. At the same time the expanding United States was moving westward toward those Mexican provinces. In 1846 the matter came to a head in both Texas and California, and as a result of the ensuing war, the United States acquired San Diego. The actual on-site takeover occurred around noon of July 29, 1846, when sailors from the American sloop-of-war, U.S.S. *Cyane*, raised the stars and stripes over the sleepy village.

The American takeover meant much to the city. It brought tremendous activity into the nascent city, with the influx of new people, energy and an entrepreneurial spirit, although not all of

This heroic statue in Presidio Park honors the Mormon Battalion composed of three hundred Mormons from Council Bluffs, Iowa, who in 1846 marched across the country to San Diego to fight in the Mexican War. While in San Diego the Mormons were highly praised. One United States official described their stay in San Diego in this ethnocentric way: "Mormons...have by a correct course of conduct become very popular with the people, and by their industry have taught the inhabitants the value of having an American population among them, and if they are continued they will be of more value in reconciling the people to the change of government than a host of Bayonets...." He pointed out that they made bricks, dug eight or ten wells in a town often without potable water, and were working on a brick courthouse. He explained that for "miles of the place the inhabitants of every rancho asked permission for some of the good Mormons to come and work for them...." Photograph from the author's collection

One of the best views of American Old Town is this sketch done in 1856 by itinerant artist Henry Miller. He traveled through California making views of cities and missions, with plans to make panoramas and an album. A San Diegan writing about him noted that Miller traveled alone and camped out every night—always placing a hair rope around his camp in order to keep out snakes. When Miller's 1856 view is compared to Stanley's 1846 drawing on page 30 one can clearly see how the town had grown in ten years, with the addition of multistoried buildings around the plaza. Photograph courtesy of The Bancroft Library, University of California, Berkeley

the activity led to immediate success. By 1860 the town still only had a population of 731, and by 1870 only a little over 2,000—and many of them were moving to Alonzo Horton's new location down by the bayside. It also did not immediately become a garden spot. One 1855 traveller said San Diego "was a most desolate looking landscape. The hills were brown and barren; not a tree or green thing was to be seen.... The prospect as we neared the town was not encouraging, but the climax was reached when we arrived at the plaza. Of all the dilapidated, miserable looking places I had ever seen, this was the worst...." This was not an isolated appraisal of American Old Town!

Much of the energy of the new occupation was provided by the military or other government officials. The fighting by the military had not been too extensive. On October 30, 1846, Commodore Robert Stockton built an earthen barrier on Presidio Hill (called ever since Fort Stockton), which was never used in combat. In the meantime two groups of armed men arrived in San Diego after marching half way across the continent. One group was the Mormon Battalion under Lt. Col. Phillip St. George Cooke. They arrived after literally cutting their way through part of the mountains, and proceeded to make themselves very useful in San Diego, although they fought no battles here. The other was a group of three hundred dragoons commanded by Brig. Gen. Stephen W. Kearny, who came from Santa Fe. They were met outside of town by a group of loyal Mexicans and defeated on December 6, 1846, in the only major battle ever fought in the area, the Battle of San Pasqual. Kearny was rescued by a relief column and came on into town. There were no other engagements in the area during the Mexican War, although troops were stationed at the old mission and a depot was established on the Bay. After the war, the military was escort to the commission charting the exact boundary between the United States and Mexico. It was culturally, socially, and economically that the military made a grand mark on San Diego in the 1840s and 1850s.

Besides Kearny, the military contingent in San Diego included some extraordinarily lively men, many of whom went on to fame in later years: George H. Derby, William H. Emory, Andrew B. Gray, W. S. Ketchum, Nathaniel Lyon, John B. Magruder, Justus McKinstry, Eugene B. Pendleton, Thomas Sweeny, Amiel W. Whipple, Cave J. Couts, Samuel DuPont, and others. Many engaged in business enterprises while in town, and a large number purchased property here, which they often continued to own long after they moved on. A number married San Diego women—Couts's marriage to Ysidora Bandini being a prime example—and a number resigned from the military to stay here permanently. They greatly stimualted the social life of the little town. One, George Horatio Derby, wrote spritely satirical pieces under the pen name *John Phoenix,* which were later published in the East and brought national attention to San Diego. The army men also organized dances, theatrical productions, and even a yacht club complete with regattas.

As historian Mario T. Garcia has explained, the most important change the Americans brought to town was the development of commerce. Trade had been stifled by Spanish regulations, which had been modified only slightly by the Mexican government. American commerce was built around sale of goods to the United States Army, trade with the ranches, and international shipping which made San Diego a regular port of call, plus the service industries needed to support it all. This led to the building of stores, hotels, saloons, boarding houses, ship chandleries, and lumber and construction firms.

The major impediment to more extensive commerce was the location of the town. It was somewhat inland from the bay, and goods had to be unloaded beach side at Point Loma (an area called La Playa) and then carted several miles to the town. It was obvious a townsite closer to the navigable water would be a boon to further development. A San Francisco speculator-businessman, William Heath Davis, recognized that and tried to develop a "New Town" at a site which would eventually be the downtown of modern San Diego. With local investors such as Californio Jose Estudillo and military men like Andrew Gray, he surveyed the land, began a deepwater wharf eleven hundred feet long, and tried to get San Diego to move. Stores, a newspaper, hotels, an army barracks, and some residences were built in the new townsite, but the plan to relocate San Diego did not come to realization—at least not then. The wharf was damaged by a shipping accident; businesses finally closed up and moved back to Old Town and within less than two years New Town was mostly deserted and would remain so until Alonzo Horton arrived in 1867. Why did the move fail in 1851 and 1852? Davis's biographer, Andrew Rolle, thinks Indian hostilities, the lack of drinking water, rivalries with La Playa and Old Town, and lack of support within the town made many reluctant to move to the new site.

Although the move to a bayside site did not work in the 1850s, other aids to commerce and a fuller community life did come into being. To assist shipping, the United States built a lighthouse on Point Loma. In 1852 regular stagecoach service to Los Angeles began, with mail service from the East coming a few years later. Scheduled steamship service supplemented the irregular commercial shipping which called at the port. Gold and copper mining in Baja provided some stimulation for the economy, although coal mining on Point Loma turned out not to. There was a continuation of fishing, a little whaling, and harvesting of sea otters. The thing that would most boost the economic enterprise of the area would have been a railroad link to the East, and efforts to

bring that about began in 1854 when the San Diego and Gila Southern Pacific and Atlantic Railroad Company was established with many prominent locals as investors. That enterprise failed for many reasons, and it would be a generation before all rail connections came to town.

Another important development after the American takeover was the decline in importance of the Californios—the Spanish-Mexican citizens. They were rather quickly eliminated from the political scene. Most also found themselves being left behind economically. The tax rolls of 1850 showed a number of well-off Californios—the Aguirres, Estudillos, Marrons, Pedrorenas, Osunas—and showed that on the average property holdings of those with Spanish surnames exceeded the property of Anglos by a margin of about four to one. Within a decade, the wealth of the Anglos exceeded that of the Hispanics. Much of the economic decline of the old families came as a result of the difficulties faced by the ranches in the period. Ranching suffered some from Indian raids and general lawlessness; high costs of food, supplies and transportation; depleted herds (there had been twenty-five thousand cattle in the county in the 1840s; only eighty-one hundred by 1855), and most especially, American law. Congress passed two laws to enable former Mexican citizens to retain their land titles if they could prove them. The process, however, was heavily weighted against the Mexicans and many lost their ranchos between 1846 and 1856. The intense racial and ethnic prejudice of the new Americans further sped the decline of Californios as a dominant force in San Diego.

The status of the Indian population also changed. As Anglos became more important in town, Indians were more and more excluded and finally were pushed into the Backcountry where they usually worked as vaqueros or laborers on the ranches, or struggled to survive on their own small land holdings. Not until the twentieth century would a

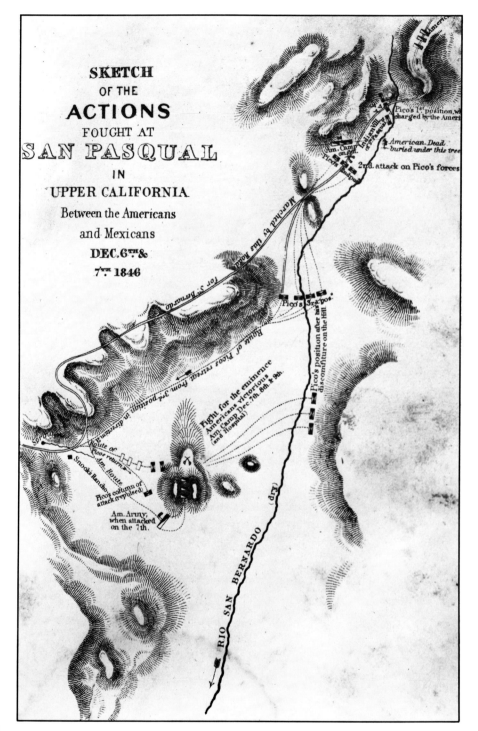

SKETCH OF THE ACTIONS FOUGHT AT SAN PASQUAL IN UPPER CALIFORNIA

Between the Americans and Mexicans

DEC. 6TH & 7TH 1846

sizable number of Indians live again in the city of San Diego.

After a quarter century of American rule, San Diego was still only a small town of something over two thousand population, located at the foot of Presidio Hill, with a more-or-less abandoned New Town south along the bay, and La Playa and the federal customhouse several miles to the west. San Diego cannot be said to have been a terribly successful enterprise to date, but all that was going to change dramatically when that archetype of the entrepreneurial-speculator, Alonzo E. Horton, came to town in 1867.

The major military engagement in San Diego during the Mexican War was the Battle of San Pasqual fought on December 6, 1846, with subsequent action on Mule Hill the next day. The battle consisted of loyal Mexican lancers trying to turn back the American dragoons under Stephen W. Kearny (who had marched to San Diego from Santa Fe) in the San Pasqual Valley east of town. The Mexicans won the battle and inflicted severe casualties on the American troops. A relief column saved the Americans who marched on into San Diego and eventually went on to participate in other engagements. The action on the battlefield can be traced in this contemporary map. Photograph courtesy of the San Diego Historical Society—Ticor Collection

William H. Emory came to San Diego as chief astronomer with the United States Boundary Commission. He shared the vision of Gray and Davis and invested heavily in Davis's New Town project, as well as another one (called Middletown) between Old Town and Davis's site. Emory was also very active in the efforts to bring the western terminus of a railroad to San Diego. Although he did not return to San Diego after 1850, he retained his San Diego real estate holdings, selling pieces off occasionally prior to his death in 1887.

Sgt. Richard Kerren was stationed in San Diego from 1850 until his death when thrown from a horse in 1856. He lived first at La Playa and then at the old mission. Kerren and his wife were active socially, especially in the theatrical productions at the mission. For instance, Victoria Jacobs, whose diary (edited by Sylvia Arden) provides much information about the period, mentions staying overnight at their quarters. Kerren was also active in local business, having dealings with local merchant Maurice Franklin, as agent for Pio Pico, and securing title to a number of lots in each part of San Diego, plus considerable livestock. Emily Wilt wrote in a recent article that "Richard Kerren became a rich, if not totally honest, San Diego pioneer."

A co-founder of New Town was Capt. Andrew B. Gray. A cultured Southerner, he served with the Texas navy and fought the Indians on the Texas plains; after leaving San Diego he was killed in the service of the Confederate States of America. He came to San Diego in 1848 as head surveyor of the United States Boundary Commission. That commission established its camp on the site Davis chose for his New Town. Davis's biographer credits Gray with visualizing a new American San Diego on that site and of calling the place to Davis's attention. In that enterprise to establish a new San Diego, Gray served as major investor, surveyor, and mapmaker. Even after leaving the area he continued to be involved, serving as agent for the project and trying to get the government to establish as many offices as possible there.

One of the most dashing military figures was George Horatio Derby, shown here at age twenty-one just a few years before coming to San Diego in 1853 as an army engineer. While here Derby also bought land, entered into business partnerships, and was involved with the *San Diego Herald*. His most notable contributions, however, were humorous writings, first under the name of *Squibob*, but later as *John Phoenix*. His sketches, puns, and jokes, often illustrated with his own drawings, delighted San Diegans and in 1855 were brought out in a book form as *Phoenixiana*. The book went through many editions and brought some national recognition to San Diego. Derby left town in 1856 and died in 1861 of poor health made worse by hard drink.

A native of Cincinnati, Oliver Spencer Witherby was a college graduate, member of the bar and officer during the Mexican War. He came to San Diego on June 1, 1849, as quartermaster and commissary officer of the United States Boundary Commission. After the commission's work was done, he returned to San Diego and began a legal and political career of note. He was appointed first judge of the new First District Court in 1850 and later served as collector of customs of the port. Witherby remained active in the local bar, and in ranching and real estate, until his death in 1896. He was fond of a good time and it has been noted that he "often went to town 'in his underwear and drawers, so drunk he didn't know what he was doing.'" When sober, he could often be seen sitting in front of his house dressed only in red flannels.

John Bankhead Magruder, shown here in an illustration from William Smythe's *History of San Diego* (1908) was a stereotypical Virginia aristocrat. He was in San Diego to command the troops at the San Diego Mission and as such was involved in the Garra Indian uprising in 1851. He went on to fame as a Confederate officer in the Civil War, winning the first Southern victory (Big Bethel Church), and fighting on the Virginia peninsula and in Texas. After the war Magruder fought for Emperor Maximilian in Mexico. When he died in 1871 Magruder still owned eleven lots in San Diego and a part of Rancho Jamacha, which he had bought into with Maj. Eugene Pendleton and Asher R. Eddy.

One of the best known military figures who came and stayed was Cave Johnson Couts, a West Pointer out of Tennessee. He is one of the best known because of his colorful personality, his importance in the social-economic political scene, and because of the prodigious collection of diaries, letters and papers (over sixteen thousand items) he left behind. Couts first came to San Diego in 1848 as escort to the surveying party of the United States Boundary Commission. He married Ysidora Bandini of one of the most distinguished Californio families, and became a major land-holder in the area. The centerpiece of his holdings was Rancho Guajome which became a major social and economic center for the northern part of the county; for instance it was one of the places Helen Hunt Jackson stayed while doing "research" for her novel *Ramona*. This photograph shows Couts (fifth from the left) and his large family in the patio of Rancho Guajome, probably in the 1860s.

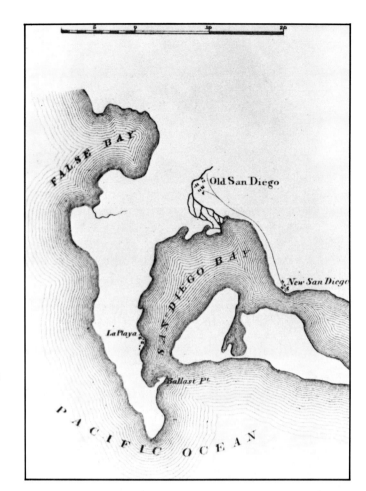

This 1853 map by army surveyor George Horatio Derby shows the locations of Old Town, at the foot of Presidio Hill; Davis's New Town, several miles south; and La Playa, the port area prior to the moving of the city to its present location. Not shown on Derby's map was another abortive subdivision, "Middletown," located about halfway between Old San Diego and New San Diego.

La Playa had been used as the loading/unloading site for decades, and the federal customhouse was located there. Previously the hide houses had been there. By the middle 1850s the area had begun to be taken over by whalers, scavengers, and other colorful characters. When Richard Henry Dana visited in 1859, all traces of the hide houses were gone and La Playa had ceased to be an important part of the town. Map courtesy of the San Diego Historical Society Research Archives

One of the navigational improvements the Americans made was the erection of a lighthouse on Point Loma. It was begun in 1854 with brick, cement, lime and lumber brought from San Francisco; that was supplemented by local sand and tiles from the abandoned Fort Guijarros. In 1855 the first keeper, James Keating, lit the wick on the lamp which could be seen thirty-nine miles out to sea. It was replaced in 1891 by a new light at the tip of Point Loma, and the old lighthouse went into decay until many years later. In 1913 the lighthouse was made the core of the Cabrillo National Monument. This view of the lighthouse probably dates from 1855, and clearly shows its position on the top of the tip of Point Loma. Photograph courtesy of the Cabrillo National Monument

Speculator and near-founder of modern San Diego, William Heath Davis passed briefly through San Diego during his long career as a California-Hawaii businessman. After successfully making a fortune in San Francisco, Davis became attracted to San Diego which he envisioned as becoming a major city. He enlisted local support and tried to move the city from its old Spanish-Mexican location to a better one near the Punto de los Muertos (at the foot of present day Market Street). Had he succeeded, Davis, and not Alonzo Horton, would have been revered as the real founder of the modern city. He is shown here in 1850, the year he came to San Diego and launched his New Town project. Photograph courtesy of the San Diego Historical Society—Ticor Collection

Because of the difficult land access, San Diego's main connection to the rest of the world was for a long time by sea. Although ships occasionally stopped at the bay, regularly scheduled steamship service only began in 1851. Soon after that the Pacific Mail Steamship Company began to serve San Diego, bringing regular mail delivery with it. These steamships brought merchandise for the stores and ranches, trade goods for the merchants, building supplies, passengers, and other essentials. For example, Victoria Jacobs noted in her diary that the steamer *Active* had just arrived, bringing her corsets. The two steamboats most frequently serving San Diego were the Pacific Mail Steamship's *Senator* and *Orizaba*. This photograph shows the *Orizaba* which served on the San Diego-San Francisco route from 1865 to 1886. Photograph courtesy of the San Diego Historical Society—Ticor Collection

SAN DIEGO HERALD.

VOL. 1. SAN DIEGO, CAL., THURSDAY, MAY 29, 1851. NO. 1.

THE SAN DIEGO HERALD.

J. JUDSON AMES,
Editor and Publisher.

OFFICE—OVER HOOPER & CO'S STORE.

The HERALD will be published every Thursday, at 10$
per annum—half in advance.

TERMS OF ADVERTISING:—One square of eight lines,
or less, first insertion, $3; each subsequent insertion 2$.
Business and address cards inserted monthly at reasonable rates.

A liberal discount made to yearly advertisers.

SAN FRANCISCO ADV'S.

DEWITT & HARRISON,
SANSOME STREET,
SAN FRANCISCO.

INVITE the attention of Merchants of Los
Angeles, Santa Barbara, San Diego and vicinity to the largest stock of general merchandise ever offered in California, all of their own
importation and selected with especial reference
to the trade of this section of the country.

15 cases rich fig'd silks; black watered and
plain blk silks,
5 cases rich fig'd silk tissues for ball and
party dresses,
5 cases emb'd muslin robes and fig'd Swiss
muslins,
3 cases fancy col'd tarlatan muslins,
5 " printed muslins and fonlard silks for
dresses,
200 cases light fancy prints, in madder col's,
of the most attractive styles,
50 cases blue and white and blue and orange
prints, extra qualities,
25 cases super qualities blue drills,
100 bales brown india drills,
25 cases bleached sheetings 4-4 to 10-4,
25 bales brown sheetings,
5 cases emb'd and plain white silk hose, extra qualities,
5 cases white and col'd cotton and lisle
thread hose for ladies and gent's,
5 cases silk, lisle thread and kid gloves and
ladies emb'd mitts,
10 cases French fonlard silk pocket hkfs, for
Mexican trade,
5 cases rich emb'd and plain French lawn
and cambric hkfs,
200 cases mens hats, of soft brush, cassi-
mere, wool and silk,
200 cases boots and brogans of French calf,
kip, goat and russett,
25 cases French cloths, super qualities, scarlet, black, blue and green,
100 bales blankets, blue scarlet white and
green,
10 cases blk silk trimming laces, for flounces,
5 cases wide white trimming laces, expressly
adapted to Mexican trade,
10 cases plain white Swiss muslins, book
muslins &c.,
5 cases rich drapery muslins, lace curtains,
5 " emb'd muslin capes, emb'd muslin
collars,
5 cases extra rich blk silk lace shawls, veils
and capes,
100 cases mens clothing, comprising every
variety and quality of new spring styles,
25 cases white muslin and calico shirts, ass'd
qualities,
50 bales blue and scarlet flannel and merino
shirts,
5 cases extra fine silk stitched blue and scarlet fancy flannel over shirts,
25 cases new styles German oil cloth and
table covers, extra qualities,
100 bales carpets and druggets, ingrain, three
ply and venitian,
10 cases Irish linens, linen toweling &c.
50 " ginghams, furniture and aproncheeks
10 " blk plain and fig'd alpacas,
100 bales seamless bags,
50 " linen bagging,
100 " Manilla rope, assorted sizes,
500 cases claret wine,
500 baskets champagne wine, best brands,
200 cases old sherry wine,
300 " old London Dock port wine,
1000 " champagne and claret cider,
1000 " pale India ale,
500 " brandied fruits, cherries, apricots &c
200 " sardines in oil,
500 " lemon syrup and raspberry syrup,
100 " Havana segars, regalias, of the very
best brands,
150 bales leaf tobacco,
100 cases chewing tobacco, in small boxes,
500 " best sperm candles,
5 0 " adamantine candles.   m29 em*

WELLS & CO.,

BANKERS, corner of Clay and Montgomery
streets, draw bills on Wells & co, Boston;
Drew, Robinson & co, New York; Ludlow,
Bebee & co, Philadelphia; Greenway & co,
Baltimore; Ellis & Morton, Cincinnati; Loker,
Renick & co, St. Louis; H. A. Rathbone, New
Orleans; Robinson & co, Buffalo; Washburn
& co, Albany; Maclean, Morris & co London;
and on banks at Hartford, New Haven, New
London, Providence, Plymouth, New Bedford,
Worcester, Salem, Portsmouth, Portland, Ban-
gor, Concord, Keene, Woodstock and Bellows
Falls.

Treasure shipped and insured to New York,
on open policies of the Boston and New York
offices to the amount of $200,000 by any one
steamer.   m29 am*

SAN FRANCISCO ADV'S.

**HARDWARE AND HOUSE FURN-
ISHING GOODS.**

ALL descriptions of the above, with builders
and mechanics tools, cut and wrought
nails, spikes,
Brittania ware, candle sticks,
Lamps, chandeliers, rich patterns;
Door locks, screws butt-hinges,
Platform scales, spring balances,
Simmons' shears, snips &c,
Solder, paint, dusting and scrub brushes,
Feather dusters, waiters and trays,
Gauging and wantage rods,
Board rules, yard sticks,
Circular and hand saws, &c, &c, &c.
For sale by.   DAVIS & CO.
Washington st, between Montgomery
and Sansome, San Francisco.
All orders left with Messrs. DILLON & Co.,
San Diego, will meet with prompt attention.
m29 tf*   D. & Co.

**TO MINERS.
UNITED STATES ASSAY OFFICE,**
SAN FRANCISCO.

MINERS are informed that this Office was
established by Congress with a view to
afford them the actual value of their Gold Dust.
When free from sand or quartz, it will yield
you from seventeen to eighteen dollars per
ounce!

We are authorized by the government, under
the supervision of an Assayer, appointed by the
President and Senate of the United States, and
have given heavy bonds for the faithful dis-
charge of our duties.

You may now realize the full value of your
labors.

GOLD DUST Received on Deposit and
safely secured in a Fire and Thief Proof Vault,
free of charge.   MOFFAT & CO.,
Montgomery, between Clay and
m29 am*   Commercial streets.

JONES' HOTEL,
SAN FRANCISCO, CALIFORNIA.

THE Location of this Hotel, at the corner of California and Sansome streets, being in the business portion of the city,
and in the immediate vicinity of the steamboat
landings, renders it a convenient resort for the
traveling public.

The building and furniture are new, and furn-
ished with a view to elegance and comfort,
making it also desirable as a permanent home
for families and single gentlemen.

The table and every other department will
receive the personal attention of the proprietor,
whose experience in the business can but insure
the comfort of its patrons.

Wines and Liquors, of the choicest brands,
to be had at the bar.   m29 am*

FURNITURE! FURNITURE!!

JUST received and now opening, per
different arrivals from New York, Boston
and Europe, the largest and best selected as-
sortments of Furniture ever brought to this
market, consisting of
Sofas,   Sideboards,
Bureaus,   Looking Glasses,
Tables of all kinds, Chairs, moh'y parlor,
Bedsteads,   do   do rock and
Washstands,   others,
Mattrasses,   do   Cane and Wood
                      do Office,
Complete setts of Chamber Furniture.
Also—magnificent plush furniture and other
articles too numerous to mention.

Families furnishing their houses, and merchants replenishing their stocks, will do well to
call upon the undersigned, where they will find
the quantity, quality and prices to suit.
                        G. O. WHITNEY.
Sacramento st., cor. of Webb st.,
between Montgomery and Kearny.
San Francisco April 10, 1851.   m29 tf f

HEDLEY & COZZENS,
SAN FRANCISCO,

OFFER for sale, in lots to suit purchasers,
1000 qr bbls clear pork,
300 " mess do
350 cases brandy,
200,000 m Havana segars, various brands,
150,000 " im regalias,
200 cases boots and shoes,
100 qr casks port wine,
10 kegs Madeira,
30 " sherry,
50 cases wild cherry brandy,
250 baskets champagne,
10 qr casks O D & Co brandy.
m29 tf f

WHOLESALE DRY GOODS.

TAAFFE & McCAHILL have removed to
the iron warehouse at the corner of Sacramento and Montgomery streets, where they
continue to keep constantly on hand the largest
assortment of Dry Goods to be found in California or Oregon.

Country merchants will find it to their advantage to call at this establishment before pur-
chasing, as we have made such arrangements
as will enable us to sell at a much lower rate
than others in the trade.   m29 am*

THE HERALD.

We make the following extract from a sweet
little poem, written by our talented young
friend M. F. Bigny, which we find in a recent
number of the New Orleans Delta.

It is entitled The Clouded Star, the Hidden
Flower, and the Broken Vow. We regret
that we have not room for the whole poem.

By a river I sat in a musing mood,
And autumnal leaves were around me strewed,
And mournful and blighted with wasting grief,
Which mocked at the thought that would ask relief,
A man appeared,—and the lines of care,
And the deeper traces of 'dull despair,'
Which darkened his youthful brow, gave me
A look of pitying sympathy.
I asked of the stranger his cause of grief—
If his sorrow were such as disdained relief—
And he told me the tale of his trustful life:
Of the maid who had promised to be his wife—
Of the damning curse of a broken vow,
Which had written distress on his youthful brow,
"But Hope," he said, and aloud he grieved,
"Is not for the heart that has been deceived:
No future trust can again unshroud
The star that is covered with falsehood's cloud;
Can never emerge from its cheerless night;
And the heart, which has worshiped a worthless thing,
Is a winter of storms which can know no spring."

Extensive Farming Operations.

The most extensive farming operation probably ever entered into in any country, has been
successfully carried through in California during
the past autumn and winter. We allude to
the speculation of Horner & Co.

Mr. Horner's Rancho is situated in the San
Jose valley. It contains 1000 acres of land
and is enclosed by an iron fence which alone
cost $10,000. Last autumn three hundred
acres only were under cultivation, two hundred
and fifty of which were planted in potatoes, the
rest in turnips, tomatoes, onions &c.

Day before yesterday the last sack of the potato crop was sold, and the gross proceeds of
this crop have amounted to $178,000. There
have been eighty hands employed on the Rancho, and the total expense of carrying it on during the season has been $80,000. The sacks
in which the potatoes have been shipped cost
over $8,000, while the gross receipts for the
total crop of the rancho have amounted to
$223,000.

This season the entire 100 acres are under
cultivation, six hundred and fifty being planted
in potatoes and the remainder in other vegeta-
bles.

Mr. Horner will doubtless be enabled to mo-
nopolize the potato trade for the next twelve
months. We have seen in one of the eastern
papers, an estimate made of the probable sales
of this potato crop when it was first planted.
This writer judged that they would amount to
$175,000; and to show how close the calcula-
tion was, had it not been for the recent fires
and the rise of potatoes, the extra $3,000
making $178,000 the actual receipts, would
not have been made.—Sacramento Trans.

Mr. Stillman lately brought into our office
a piece of wood taken from a cayota hole
on Lawson's hill, sixty-two feet below the
surface. It is beautifully encrusted in pieces with sulphate of iron, and is a great cu-
riosity.—Nevada Gazette.

We were recently shown a lump of gold
weighing 8lbs. 8oz., taken out of Poor Man's
Creek a few days since by Mr. T. Turner,
brother of Mr. Turner of the Nevada Hotel
in this city. It was taken from the bed of
the creek.—Ib.

THE HANGING OF McCAULEY—McCauley
was hung in his cell during Thursday night, as
we announced yesterday. Gov. McDougal had
concluded to commute the sentence to impri-
sonment, and arrived at Benicia on Thursday,
just in time to issue the commutation, so that
it could reach Napa on Friday morning before
the execution should take place. A few of the
citizens of Napa, who happened to be in Benicia on Thursday evening, when they heard that
the commutation had actually been issued, took
horses and proceeded to Napa, and during the
night or Friday morning before daybreak, Mc-
Cauley's cell was entered, a spike was driven
into a beam, and this prisoner was deliberately
executed. The next morning, when the cell
was entered, the body was found still hanging.
—Ib.

Another mark of the American invigoration of San Diego was the introduction of the town's first newspaper on May 29, 1851. It was published by a huge and colorful personage, 300-pound John Judson Ames. A New Englander whose career as a sailor ended after he was convicted for manslaughter, Ames then went into newspaper work in several locations, ending up in San Diego in 1850. He brought the printing equipment from New Orleans (with horrible adventures on the Isthmus of Panama when the press fell into the Charges River at one point). Ames first began publishing in Davis's New Town, but when that failed, moved to Old Town, where he continued publishing until 1860 when a gold discovery near San Bernardino lured him and his press to that town. This photograph of the first issue's front page gives an idea of a typical copy of the *Herald*. Photograph courtesy of the San Diego Historical Society—Ticor Collection

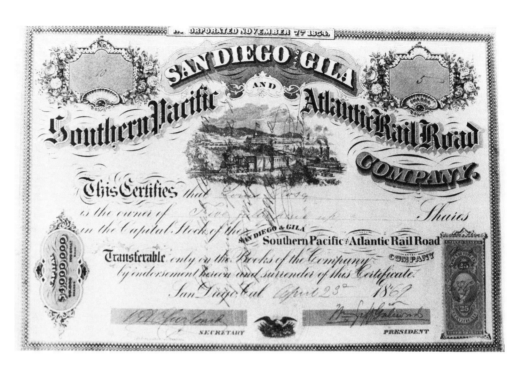

Still another "improvement" the Americans brought to San Diego was education. Although the mission had provided some schooling for Indians, there was little other education available in the Spanish-Mexican period of San Diego. For instance, in 1845 only eleven of twenty-five voters could write. The Americans established schools almost immediately upon their arrival. They did not flourish without controversy, however. Mary Chase Walker, a Yankee schoolmarm, was engulfed in a major racial incident in 1866. She took a quadroon woman to lunch in the Franklin House dining room. The town was scandalized and parents removed their children from her class and besieged the school trustees with complaints. The incident reminds us of the extensive racism of the mid-nineteenth century. In San Diego such racism was directed at the tiny Afro-American population, at the Native Americans, and at the Californios. Photograph courtesy of the San Diego Historical Society—Ticor Collection

The dream of a railroad to San Diego began early. Before the Civil War there was hope San Diego would be the terminus of the southern route of the transcontinental railroad. A number of San Diegans formed the San Diego Gila Southern Pacific and Atlantic Company to hurry the process along by building a railroad from San Diego to the Colorado River at the mouth of the Gila River. Although the company was around for years, nothing came of the project, and it was many years before a railroad came to San Diego. The above stock certificate was owned by Louis Rose, one of the early investors and the first Jewish citizen to move to San Diego. Photograph courtesy of the San Diego Historical Society Research Archives

Although the sea remained the main avenue into San Diego for a long time, the Americans did improve ground transportation and communication. The first regular stage service to Los Angeles began in 1851, and service to the east began in 1857. This was the "Jackass Mail" stage line between San Antonio and San Diego, which was made possible by a congressional subsidy to provide mail service. The opening of the line was so popular that it created a crisis in the town—the post office ran out of stamps and envelopes! The Jackass Mail was discontinued in 1861 with the Civil War, and the later Butterfield Stage system bypassed San Diego, leaving the town in its normal isolated state. The first mail brought on the Jackass Mail was carried on packhorses, but in time stages, like the one shown above in the Backcountry, were added and passengers and some freight were also carried. Service was primitive with little attention paid to passenger comfort. Photograph courtesy of the San Diego Historical Society—Ticor Collection

Louis Rose (photographed in 1870) came to San Diego in 1850. He was the first of a sizable and significant Jewish population in American Old Town. In its frontier environment, San Diego Christians and Jews seemed to have maintained good business and social relations. Rose was involved in business and real estate and Roseville and Rose Canyon were named after him. Other prominent Jewish citizens of the period were Lewis and Maurice Franklin; the Mannasse family; the Jacobs family, whose daughter Victoria left a diary which illustrates the easy Jewish-Gentile relations of the 1850s; and Marcus Katz, whose marriage to Leah Jacobs was probably the first Jewish wedding in Southern California. The only major conflict occurred in 1859 during Yom Kippur. Local Jewish males were performing sacred services when law officers interrupted to bring Moses Mannasse before the county grand jury to testify regarding an incident he had witnessed. The disruption of the Jewish services led to a national debate among the Jewish citizens of the country over the proper obligations of Jews to civil authority. It was one of the few times San Diego made the national press in this period. Photograph courtesy of the San Diego Historical Society—Ticor Collection

In 1853 San Diego had a famous murder trial and execution. It began when Lt. Col. Louis S. Craig, commander of an escort with the United States Boundary Commission, was apparently murdered by two deserters, Acting Corporal William Hays and a Private Condon. The men were apprehended by Indians, brought to the Army, court-martialed and found guilty of murder. The execution took place at the Army camp in the old mission January 31, 1853. The commander, John B. Magruder, staged a dramatic event, with Indians, the infantry, artillery, and a delegation of officials from town all lined at dress parade. At noon a cart bearing the prisoners, dressed only in white shrouds and sitting on their coffins, pulled up to the scaffold. After each prisoner said a few appropriate words, the trap was sprung and a half-hour later the bodies were cut down and buried. Photograph from the *Illustrated News* April 2, 1853

With the breakup of the missions in the Mexican period, and the further deterioration of the Indian position after the American conquest, most Indians in San Diego were squeezed out of town and into the countryside or into *rancherias* on the edge of town. A study by Alexandra Luberski shows that by 1870 there were virtually no Indian servants working in San Diego, although there had been earlier. The dissatisfaction of the Indians with their status was shown by the continual strife and bloodshed, which reached its peak in 1851 with the Garra Revolt. Perhaps because of the white prejudices and the Indian hostilities, there are few illustrations of the native population of San Diego during the American Old Town period. One of the few was by Arthur Schott showing a Kumeyaay family near Warner Springs. Illustration from William H. Emory, *Report on the United States and Mexican Survey* (1857)

One of the best photographs of American Old Town was this one, taken in the 1870s. It shows the southern end of the plaza, with flagpole, cannons, and some citizens in the foreground. The buildings include, left to right, the frame house of George A. Johnson, the Casa Bandini (at that time serving as the Cosmopolitan Hotel), and the Casa Estudillo. In the background with the windmill is Seeley Stables, built in the early 1860s, to serve the stage lines. Notice the barren nature of the plaza itself, and the hillsides behind. San Diego is, in its natural form, a desert, and most plants currently in the city have been planted by recent arrivals and are watered with imported water. Photo courtesy of The Bancroft Library, University of California, Berkeley

M. of San Diego.

The Civil War had little impact on San Diego. Most of what did occur took place at the Army barracks in otherwise deserted New Town, where California Volunteers were stationed during most of the war. One of them, Eli Warnock Hazen, described the situation as follows: "This is a most healthy post but a very expensive one to government. . . . it is situated on the north bank of San Diego Bay about three miles from Old San Diego from which all the water used at the barracks has to be hauled in a wagon drawn by government mules, wood used is hauled a distance varrying [sic] from fifteen to fourty [sic] miles at great expense. As a means of defense it is utterly usless [sic] and should be abandoned." The only part of his description which is suspect is the comment concerning firewood; local residents say that the Volunteers stripped the abandoned houses and tore down the remains of Davis's wharf for firewood. The 1850 barracks remained a part of the San Diego scene well into the twentieth century; this photograph shows the building a few years after Hazen's description. Photograph courtesy of the San Diego Historical Society— Ticor Collection

Although the barracks in New Town were the focal point for troops in San Diego during the Civil War, the old mission was also used as a military base. That can clearly be seen in this sketch by Henry Miller made during an 1850 sojourn in San Diego. As he noted in *Tour of the California Missions*, "The mission buildings have lost their ancient appearance, having been renovated by the government, and serve now as the quarters of United States troops. . . . Being built on an elevation, it offers a fine view; below it are numerous olive trees, together with some palm and fruit trees." In addition to serving as a base for troops, the old mission played a role in the social life of the period as well. In her 1856 diary, Victoria Jacobs mentions occasional rides and picnics to the site, and even staying overnight after theatrical productions. Photograph courtesy of The Bancroft Library, University of California, Berkeley

This J. Henfield photograph of 1869 is one of the earliest and most reproduced views of the town. It shows San Diego in 1869, just as Alonzo Horton was beginning his campaign to move the town down the Bay; as such it captures Old Town San Diego at its peak. The picture shows such new enterprises as a brick courthouse, the Daley Match Factory, and many new commercial buildings which had appeared after the American takeover in 1846. Photograph courtesy of the California State Library.

3

Alonzo Horton's New San Diego

1867-1889

O n April 15, 1867, Alonzo E. Horton stepped off the steamer into the little boat which would bring him to terra firma in what was then called (often in derision) "Davis's New Town." A distinguished looking man with a fertile mind, Horton brought with him money and experience as a speculator and the founder of a town. He was the man who would succeed where William Heath Davis had failed; Horton would move San Diego down the bay, and there it would begin the growth and development that would make it the eighth largest city in the United States by the 1980 census.

More immediately, his arrival launched an extraordinary generation for San Diego. Between his 1867 arrival and 1890, the town would move and Old Town would wither. At the new site there would be land development, new buildings, new wharves, and modern conveniences. Population would grow to forty thousand in the boom year of 1888. There would be a tremendous real estate boom between 1886 and 1888, and there would be a large collapse in 1888 and 1889. A larger Afro-American population, a growing Chinese community, Backcountry mining and agriculture, and the development of significant cultural institutions would follow. San Diego *really* began with the arrival of Alonzo Horton in 1867!

As traced in Elizabeth MacPhail's *The New San Diego and Alonzo E. Horton*, the process began when Horton purchased a large block of land east of Davis's New Town site, had it surveyed and platted, and began to sell lots and build buildings. Success came quickly, with the new site going from twenty-three residents in 1868, to 915 occupied houses and sixty-nine commercial buildings in 1870. As the town continued to grow at the new site, it became apparent that Old Town was being bypassed. After considerable acrimony, the city government and its records were moved to the new town in 1871, and the post office there was officially designated *San Diego*. From that point on, Old Town declined (helped by a fire in 1872) and San Diego *was* the town on Horton's site.

As the town prospered, the things that make a city came to it. The newspaper moved up from Old Town in 1871. The telephone, telegraph, and electricity arrived, and the water system was improved. In 1882 a new school was built and a library established. With Horton's wharf (finished in 1869) commerce grew, and residents and speculators began to arrive. The long-hoped-for railroad connection came in 1885. Expectations of that event triggered two booms, the 1871-73 Scott Boom and the bigger 1886-88 boom.

The Scott Boom occurred when Col. Thomas Scott got Congress to charter his Texas and Pacific Railroad, which would end at San Diego. A boom immediately followed with population growing to five thousand by 1873. When the stock market collapsed that same year, Scott and the railroad went down with it. San Diego quickly shrunk back to about fifteen hundred people. But it did not die.

For one thing, the hinterland was beginning to develop. There was a gold rush beginning in 1869 which led to the establishment of mines and the new town of Julian. The mines stimulated activity in San Diego, as well as bringing development to the Backcountry. In addition, agriculture began to expand in the 1870s as people became more aware of the possibilities of the area and its mild climate. Cattle ranching began to be of less importance, but honey became a major industry, as did fruits, grains, and other cultivated crops. If railroad transportation connecting San Diego with the East would ever arrive, San Diego could become a major agricultural center.

In the mid-1880s activity speeded up, with the railroad the cause—again. After complicated and confusing maneuvers and false starts and problems, the first train connections with the rest of the nation came to town on November 15, 1885. San Diego then entered her most dramatic boom. Population soared from fifteen hundred in 1873 to around five thousand in 1885 to an estimated forty thousand in 1888. People were arriving in town at the rate of two thousand to three thousand per month on the new railroads (stimulated by fare competition), and over one thousand ships per year called at the port, bringing both passengers and supplies. Real estate prices boomed as lot prices went from $25 to $2,500 per foot front. Homes, businesses, hotels, and real estate firms were built at a furious pace. It was a spectacular boom.

While San Diego grew in population during the boom, it also expanded physically. For one thing, the development of inter-urban transportation led to the development of a number of neighborhoods within the city—La Jolla, Pacific Beach, Ocean Beach, Grantville,

The man shown in this picture is Alonzo Erastus Horton as he appeared in 1867. Father Serra notwithstanding, Horton is the real "Father" of San Diego. A New Englander by birth, he spent some years in Wisconsin, where he founded Hortonville (which did not become as successful as San Diego; as of 1980, it still had a population of only about fifteen hundred), before coming to California during the gold rush. He made considerable money in San Francisco and then began to dream of making a great city out of San Diego. He sold his San Francisco business and sailed to San Diego, arriving on April 15, 1867. It was then such a pitiful place that there was no wharf for ships and he had to be carried from ship to shore, and then after a long wait, had to take a wagon to Old San Diego. That wait for transportation was crucial; while killing time he walked around the bayside area (he was in Davis's New Town) and immediately grasped the prospects of that waterfront situation for the town. The rest, as the saying goes, is history! Photograph courtesy of the San Diego Historical Society—Ticor Collection

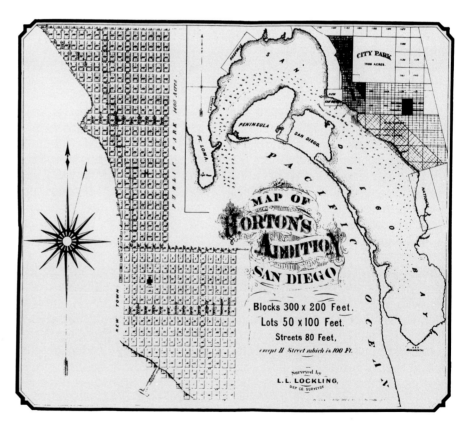

Soon after his arrival in San Diego, Horton purchased the land known as Horton's Addition. He did so after considerable maneuvering. Although the town was supposedly governed by a group of trustees (the previous town charter having been revoked), there had been no election for awhile and there was a question as to whether the current trustees had the authority to sell land to Horton. Horton and some supporters he quickly attracted arranged an election and the new trustees immediately sold him nearly a thousand acres at the average price of a few cents per acre. He had the land surveyed and platted and the *new* new town was ready for business. Horton's land was due east of Davis's *old* New Town, and continued the same regular pattern of streets Davis had established. Note that it already contains a large body of land called "Public Park," the origins of Balboa Park. This map by L. L. Locking probably dates from 1870, and is usually called the "final" and "finished" plat map for Horton's Addition. Map courtesy of the San Diego Historical Society Research Archives

and University Heights, for example. Likewise, many new towns in the county were settled (or at least laid out and promised by developers). Many of them were along railroads such as Del Mar, Encinitas, Carlsbad, Oceanside, and Escondido along the California Southern Railroad. To the east, La Mesa, El Cajon, and Lakeside emerged; and to the south, Otay, National City, and Chula Vista appeared. Across the bay Coronado began in 1885. With bands playing and caravans carrying prospective customers out to the new developments, San Diegans lived in a circus atmosphere from 1885 to 1888.

If the boom was spectacular, so was the crash. The crash did not originate in San Diego specifically, but was part of a larger Southern California pattern. As Glenn Dumke has pointed out, interest rates rose sharply and caused some to have to liquidate their holdings on short notice. When that occurred, the economy "deflated like pricked balloons." In addition, an anticipated winter tourism did not emerge as the speculators had expected. In any case, the boom ended and within a few months the population of San Diego shrank from forty thousand to about sixteen thousand.

Although the crash may have taken some of the air out of San Diego's balloon, it did not destroy the little city. Quite the contrary, the 1880s left the town with major developments in social and public services which were foundations for future growth. For instance, by the end of the period urban transportation had been improved; fire, police and sewer departments had been established and electricity had arrived. Public buildings—the courthouse and high school—were built or enlarged. Even the red-light district in the "Stingaree" grew! Also the city charter was changed to create a more responsive government, and the city offices grew so much that they had to move into new quarters in the Horton Bank Building. Some downtown streets were paved, and a sort of welfare system was begun with a new poor farm.

There were also important social and cultural foundations. A library was organized in 1882; a Women's Christian Temperance Union branch in 1884. A number of clubs and organizations—the Cuyamaca Club, the San Diego Rowing Club, and the San Diego Medical Society—were established. The City Guard Band came into being and was kept busy. There were also baseball teams and other sporting activities. Art, music, and spiritualism flourished, especially around the ethereal figure of Jesse Shepard.

Furthermore, more racial and ethnic diversity came to the city. A sizable Chinese population settled in the area to work on construction projects, as domestic servants, and as fishermen and merchants. Enough Germans came to town to support a German-language newspaper and social organizations. Although still mostly in the rural areas, Afro-Americans began to make more and more contributions to the county. Unfortunately, Indians continued to be considered second-class citizens and were kept mostly in the Backcountry, where a number of reservations were created. While the number of non-whites began to be more and more important to the community, the degree of white racial prejudice also manifested itself more vigorously, especially in hostility toward the Chinese.

The decades of the 1870s and 1880s were, then, fundamental to the emergence of San Diego. Population began to grow and basic community services, organizations, and infrastructures were established. After a couple of decades of consolidation, San Diego would be ready to begin moving forward again.

Father Antonio Ubach was a familiar figure in San Diego from his arrival in 1866 to his funeral in 1907, which was "an occasion of city-wide mourning by all faiths." Ubach worked to build the Roman Catholic church in San Diego, in civic affairs (he was very active in the efforts to bring a railroad to town, for example), and most especially, he worked to help the Indians of San Diego. His work throughout the county on behalf of the Indians brought him a national reputation, which he used to convince President Ulysses S. Grant to begin establishing reservations for some of the San Diego County Indians. This undated photograph shows Father Ubach (on the right) with some of his Indian friends at some location in the Backcountry. Photograph courtesy of the San Diego Historical Society—Ticor Collection

Horton's new site was nice, but it needed both a centerpiece and a hotel to house new arrivals and prospective buyers. Horton provided both. On January 1, 1870, he had ground broken for the Horton House, to be the most spectacular building in all of San Diego. It was called "mammoth," and "the largest building in Southern California," and had over one hundred rooms, each with walnut finishings, marble-top tables, carpeting, running water, steam heating, and magnificent views in all directions. Horton House was important; it gave confidence to the new community and encouraged others to invest here. This photograph, probably taken in 1872 when the Horton House was just completed, shows the substantial nature of the building—but also the raw and unfinished nature of the town in that year. Photograph courtesy of the San Diego Historical Society—Ticor Collection

As Horton's new site became more viable, businesses began to emerge and buildings were built to house them. This was the store Abraham Klauber and Samuel Steiner built in 1869 at Seventh and "I" Streets, the site chosen because the main road to Old Town and Los Angeles went through that intersection. It was the beginning of what was, at its dissolution in 1980, the oldest business in the city. Many other businesses also were created around this time—although most did not survive as long as Steiner and Klauber. Other firms established in the period were Thearle's Music; San Diego Federal; Marston's; Jessop and Sons; Luce, Forward, Hamilton and Scripps; Morgan Linen Company; Title Insurance and Trust Company; Union Ice Company; and Ward and Ward, Attorneys. Photograph courtesy of the Klauber Wangenheim Company

By 1870 it was obvious that San Diego had shifted from the foot of Presidio Hill to Horton's Addition. It no longer made sense to keep the government in Old Town, so on July 9, 1870, the county supervisors ordered the county records moved to the new townsite. All hell broke loose. After much confusion, the county clerk and recorder, Chalmers Scott, moved the records to the new town and a courthouse was established temporarily in the Express Building. The records were moved at night to avoid trouble with those Old Town citizens who refused to capitulate; that has given rise locally to the story that the records were stolen in the dark of the night. It is probably in the spirit of that anecdote that the 1960 reenactment of the moving of the court records was done. Photograph courtesy of the San Diego Historical Society—Ticor Collection

This somewhat fanciful 1883 etching of San Diego shows clearly one of the more important developments which led to the growth of the town after Horton's arrival—the building of wharves so ocean-going ships could service the area more effectively. The short wharf to the left was built by S. S. Culverwell at about the same location as the previous Davis Wharf. Note the barracks to the right of that wharf. The longer wharf was built by Alonzo Horton from the foot of Fifth Street, and was the real commercial center of San Diego for many years after its construction in 1869. Note also the *Orizaba* in the bay; she continued throughout this period to be the steamer which most frequently called at San Diego. Photograph courtesy of The Bancroft Library, University of California, Berkeley

In the early 1870s, when Isaiah W. Taber took this photograph, Horton's New Town was well underway. The population was over two thousand, and a sizable number of buildings had been erected. Property tax evaluations had increased tremendously, and all that was really needed to make the place a major metropolis was the railroad. Expectations of that happy event caused the Tom Scott Boom of 1873 which brought inhabitants up to five thousand, before the "Black Friday" collapse of the stock market destroyed Scott's Texas and Pacific Railroad. Photograph courtesy of The Bancroft Library, University of California, Berkeley

The previous overview of San Diego in the 1870s is supplemented by this 1870s Carleton Watkins downtown street scene. Note the preponderance of frame buildings and the rough, frontier atmosphere. This photograph is one half of a stereoscopic view which, when viewed through the machine most late-nineteenth-century parlors contained, would give a three-dimensional view of the scene. Note the way the people in the street are carefully posed in order to enhance that three dimensional effect. They are also very stiff-looking; photography at that point still took a long time and did not allow for action or candid shots. Stereoscopic photographs like this one were very popular at the time and introduced many people to the wonders of the world—China, Yosemite, Yellowstone, and the London Bridge—and new towns like San Diego which wanted to boost themselves in the eyes of the world. Photograph courtesy of the California State Library

SAN DIEGO CAL.

The *reality* of the two preceding photographs of San Diego in the 1870s contrasts sharply with the *hopes* expressed in this 1873 lithograph by George Holbrook Baker, a prominent lithographer of the period headquartered in San Francisco. The most-striking feature is the railroad which is steaming into the center of the picture. That railroad represents Tom Scott's dream of the Texas Pacific Railroad which would end in San Diego. Unfortunately, it was never built! Since there are no contemporary references to Baker, there is a question as to whether he even visited San Diego. Although it was rare for nineteenth-century lithographers to misrepresent the cities they depicted, they did sometimes, usually in views sponsored by local boosters. Photograph courtesy of San Diego Historical Society Public Library Collection

One of the things which provided support for the growth of San Diego in the 1870s was the gold rush in the mountains. As Helen Ellsberg has pointed out in her book on the Julian mines, there had been notice of gold at least as far back as 1602, but nothing happened until 1869. Then an Afro-American cattleman, A. E. (Fred) Coleman led his horse to the creek for a drink, and saw the glitter of gold. A rush followed and mines, claims, camps, and people sprouted all over the area. In 1870 some of the settlers founded the town of Julian, which became the main town of the mining area and of the Backcountry. Long after the mines dribbled out, the town has remained as a center for ranching, orchards, and tourism. This 1874 photograph shows how the town had developed within just four years. Photograph courtesy of the San Diego Historical Society—Ticor Collection

These two photographs say much about the mining boom which flourished around Julian from 1869 until the turn of the century. The first photograph shows the Eagle Mine, opened in 1870, and indicates the type of hard, individual labor which was the main feature of mining for most people. This picture, probably taken in 1870, shows Al Frary and Luther Bailey working their mine.

The other photograph shows the Stonewall Mine about 1900. It be-

came one of the largest and most successful mines in the area, and illustrates the industrial model of mining, with large and complex machinery and a large number of employees. This mine operated until a shaft cave-in occurred in 1926. Today the site is marked and some scraps of machinery can be seen within the boundaries of Cuyamaca State Park. Both photographs courtesy of the San Diego Historical Society-Ticor Collection

Julian was not important just for its mines and apples; it was also the town where many Afro-Americans first made their mark on San Diego County. The discoverer of gold, Fred Coleman, was himself an Afro-American, but his fame was soon eclipsed by Albert Robinson. Robinson was a freed slave who moved to Julian sometime around 1880 and built a restaurant and the Robinson Hotel. In the 1880 census, the black population of Julian was thirty-one and included miners, farmers, laborers, property owners, and nine school children. That constituted 60 percent of the Afro-American population in San Diego County. This undated photograph shows the most successful of San Diego County's black population in front of his hotel. Photograph courtesy of the San Diego Historical Society—Ticor Collection

It must not be forgotten that San Diego County was still a frontier in the 1870s. An incident at the Gaskill Brothers store in Campo (small village about sixty miles east of San Diego, along the Mexican border) illustrates that. Silas and Lyman Gaskill operated a store, blacksmith shop, and hotel at Campo. On December 4, 1875, a gang of seven Mexican thieves and rustlers made the mistake of attacking the Gaskills. When it was over, three of the Mexicans were dead and two were left behind wounded. One of the wounded died during the night and the other was taken to a nearby ranch, hanged and then thrown into an old well. The disorder along the border continued for some time, and finally a detachment of American cavalry was sent to the scene in 1876. Although this photograph taken by Albert Kroff is from 1903, the store (the stone building on the right) and the village itself, looked much as they had in 1875. Photograph courtesy of the Klauber Wangenheim Company

The development of agriculture in the area was another reason San Diego began to grow significantly in the 1870s and 1880s. These four drawings illustrate some of the types of crops which were becoming important to the area—alfalfa and cattle raising, vineyards, fruit orchards, and honey. The vineyards were usually in the interior valleys, planted with cuttings from abroad, and extensive enough to support four wineries and an export trade in raisins. The orchards were usually olive and deciduous fruits (which were not too successful); citrus and avocados would come later. Beekeeping became such a major industry that San Diego County was at one time the largest producer of honey in the United States. The development of all farming establishments was greatly aided by the improved transportation systems of the time. Photographs from Wallace W. Elliott, *History of San Bernardino and San Diego Counties* (1883)

The Parks Sanatorium for Tuberculosis in La Mesa illustrates yet another facet of the development of modern San Diego—the role of climate and health. From the very earliest booster propaganda, stress has been made on the climate—for agriculture, for quality of life, *and* for health. A large number of San Diego's early residents came to the town for health reasons; beginning in the 1870s health became an industry. Sanatoriums of several varieties were set up; the first was probably Dr. Peter Remondino's private hospital established in 1879. A number of hotels advertised health as one of the benefits in staying with them. Several Backcountry locations developed health centers around hot or mineral springs, and one promoter even bottled water from a spring at Jamacha for sale as a cure-all. Photograph courtesy of the San Diego Historical Society—Ticor Collection

Although some Chinese began to come to San Diego in the 1860s, most came in the 1880s and 1890s, reaching a peak in 1890 when they constituted 2.6 percent of the population. Many first worked on the railroad construction crews and others served as domestic servants, laundrymen, gardeners, and day laborers. The enterprise the Chinese were best known for in San Diego, however, was fishing. The November 8, 1885 *San Diego Union* reported that "nearly all the Chinese living in San Diego are engaged in the fishing business." That was not really true; in fact, only 10 percent were fishermen at the time. The Chinese did have a near monopoly on fishing. They sold some of their catch door-to-door and cured the rest for export to China or Chinese markets within the United States. The Chinese fishing industry was pretty much gone by 1890, possibly due to pollution in the bay, federal legislation, and the overfishing

caused by use of extremely fine meshed nets. Their vessels were junks such as we see anchored in the harbor in the 1880s. Photograph courtesy of the San Diego Historical Society—Ticor Collection

While many Chinese in San Diego were laborers, a few became affluent merchants and professional people. One was Quon Mane, shown with his family in 1903, who came to San Diego in 1881 and, in partnership with his brothers, created an import business which became quite prosperous. Like most Chinese homes and businesses, it was located in the downtown "Stingaree" area close to the harbor. The Chinese community in San Diego existed in the face of severe white hostility, which led to the fishermen being driven out of their businesses, "No Chinese Employed" signs in windows, Chinese removed from all public jobs, and continual threats of violence. San Diego did not experience the violence and bloodshed of some western communities in the era; instead Sheriff Joseph Coyne formed a "Committee of Public Safety" to protect the San Diego Chinese from local mobs. Despite their troubles, the Chinese became a permanent part of San Diego, creating community organizations and continuing to play a prominent role in the cultural and business life of the town. Photograph courtesy of the San Diego Historical Society—Ticor Collection

Whales, such as this ninety-foot behemoth on a San Diego beach, have long been important to San Diego—first for the whaling industry and more recently for the tourist industry. In the beginning Indians used what they could from beached whales; then Europeans and Americans used San Diego for "shore whaling." In the period of the 1850s through the 1870s whaling was a significant part of San Diego's economy. At its peak in 1872, San Diego produced fifty-five thousand gallons of whale oil—the equivalent to the oil of eighteen hundred whales. By the 1870s the United

States government began to drive whalers from their Point Loma grounds so that defense installations could be built. After a brief flurry of activity on North Island in the 1880s, the industry died. Photograph courtesy of the UCLA Special Collections

In a sense, this is San Diego's United States Centennial portrait. The 1876 bird's eye view was done by E. S. Glover for the A. L. Bancroft Company's series of California city views. It shows the city in considerable detail, even including outbuildings and windmills. Point Loma and the Coronado Islands are in the far background; Coronado and North Island (separated by the Spanish Bight) are in the center. The Centennial of the nation was celebrated in San Diego with great enthusiasm. There were parades, concerts, speeches, formal dinners, and even the works of the Poet of the Day, Philip Morse, who did twenty-three verses along these lines:

> Sown in a rugged soil a century
>   Ago, and nourished by the patriot's blood
> The seed has sprung, the flower of Liberty
>   Blooms out today in beauty from the bud.

Drawn by E. S. Glover and Published by Schneider & Kueppers, San Diego.

Entered according to Act of Congress, in the year 1876, b

Showing the central portion of the city, with the *actual* improvements; San Diego Bay and Peninsula, the **Entrance** to the Harbor, Point Loma, and the Los Coronados Islands, twenty miles distant in the Pacific Ocean.

1. Presbyterian Church.	5. Catholic Church.	9. Bank of San Diego.
2. Baptist Church.	6. Public Schools.	10. Commercial Bank.
3. Methodist Church.	7. Point Loma Seminary.	11. City Hall.
4. Episcopal Church.	8. San Diego Academy.	12. Central Market Building.

BIRD'S
SAN DIEGO
FROM THE NORT

IEW OF

ALIFORNIA

KING SOUTH-WEST.

The County Seat of San Diego County and the proposed Terminus of the Texas Pacific Railroad. Present Population, about 3,000. A commercial town; publishes two newspapers, "San Diego Union" and "World," weekly and daily editions.

13.	Horton's Hall.	17.	Lyon House.	21.	Book Store of Schneider & Kueppers.
14.	Telegraph Offices.	18.	Bay View Hotel.	22.	San Diego Foundry.
15.	Horton House.	19.	Government Barracks.	23.	San Diego Planing Mill.
16.	San Diego County Court House.	20.	San Diego Flouring Mill.	24.	City Brewery.

The *San Diego Union* began printing in Old Town in 1868, and as such, carries the distinction of being the city's oldest continually-operating newspaper. Like so much else, the press came to town on the steamer *Orizaba*, and was installed in a little wooden house. In 1870 the paper was successful enough to begin printing as a daily, and in 1871 it moved to Horton's New Town, after having led the hostility toward the new city for the previous three years. Its up-to-date-for-the-times printing plant is shown here as depicted in 1883. Although the *Union* became the major and most durable of the San Diego newspapers, others did flourish in the period—the *Bulletin*, the *Daily Bee*, and the *San Diego Sun*, for example. Illustration from Wallace W. Elliott, *History of San Bernardino and San Diego Counties* (1883)

San Diego's first high school was built during this period. It started as Russ School, built in 1882 with the gift of lumber from Humboldt County lumberman Joseph Russ, whose company had supplied much of the lumber to early San Diego. At first the building—shown here in an illustration from the School Board's published financial report of 1891 (with gymnasium added)—was used as a general school, but by 1893 it was devoted exclusively to high school and renamed Russ High School. The building served as the centerpiece of San Diego education until it was replaced in 1907 by a larger masonry structure called the "Gray Castle." Photograph courtesy of San Diego High School Alumni Association

The arrival of the rail connections brought a tremendous boom to San Diego from 1885 to 1888. Visitors came to the city by the thousands to buy real estate. Reception committees from the Chamber of Commerce and various realtors met each train and ship and drove the new arrivals to the hotels, homes, and tents where they would stay. Every day the streets were filled with sights like this one in 1885, as developers loaded wagons with prospective buyers and conveyed them, often to the beat of marching bands and always with lots of flags and bunting, to the irresistible real estate. Photograph courtesy of the San Diego Historical Society—Ticor Collection

Although the boom of the 1880s was exciting, it was not without its unpleasantries. For one thing, there was not enough housing. Ad Pearson remembers hundreds of small tents covering dozens of vacant lots, plus an "immense tent" at Third and "E" Streets, where one could obtain a cot with pillow and blankets for $1.50 per night. There were, however, many entertainments to take your mind off the lack of accommodations. Pearson recalls a "gambling fever" which "developed from fortunes made in real estate." There were saloons, gunmen, and if one went to Tijuana, prize fights, and bear and bull baiting. Pearson also says so many "scarlet women" were in Tijuana on weekends that it took until Tuesday or Wednesday to get them all back by train to San Diego. If these organized entertainments were not enough, a street fight could usually be found most anywhere. It was a boom town! Photograph courtesy of the San Diego Historical Society—Ticor Collection

In nineteenth-century America hotels played a major role in the cities. They were needed, especially in places like San Diego, to house the speculators and businessmen who flocked to the new urban centers. Hotels were often the most-imposing buildings in a town and frequently became social centers for the local population. In San Diego in the 1880s, many major hotels, such as the Del Coronado, were also built as resort hotels. Others were downtown hotels, like the old Horton House, the Florence Hotel, or the one shown here, the Hotel Brewster. It opened in 1888 on the corner of Fourth and "C" Streets, and was notable for the first passenger elevator in San Diego, visible to the left of the stairway. Photograph courtesy of the California State Library

With the boom of the mid-1880s, San Diego took on the appearance of a busy town, with lots of commerce. This 1885 picture of the intersection of Seventh and Ash Street shows some of the retail establishments and advertisements present in town at that time. Aggressive merchandising was clearly *not* a monopoly of the real estate developers! Photograph courtesy of the Bancroft Library, University of California, Berkeley

A busy harbor was a characteristic of San Diego in the period. With the difficulties of land transportation, the sea remained the chief means of moving people and goods. One of the major wharves was the Santa Fe Wharf, with its two wings. It was served by the railroad whose cars went out onto the wharf to receive and unload cargo. Photograph courtesy of the California State Library

It must always be remembered that the dominant form of architecture in the new San Diego was Victorian. A prime example of the more elaborate Victorian style would be Jesse Shepard's residence, the Villa Montezuma, on "K" Street. These 1887 photographs show both the exterior and a portion of the interior of the house, and illustrate the ornate decorations, woodwork, and "fussy" interior decor. This house was built by local benefactors in 1887 to attract to the city Benjamin Jesse Francis Shepard, concert pianist and friend of the arts. For a brief period of time his house was the social center of town, where music was performed, litera-ture read, and art (much of it in the house) appreciated. Shepard left after the collapse of the boom and the house fell into other uses, to be rescued in 1970 by the San Diego Historical Society which has restored it as a house museum and cultural center for the neighborhood. Both photographs courtesy of the San Diego Historical Society—Ticor Collection

Bum under the Surgeons care. 643

Architecture was not the only Victorian thing in San Diego in the 1880s; there was also a sentimental dog story. The San Diego dog was "Bum," and although not as inspirational as Edinburgh's "Greyfriars Bobby" who spent years in vigil on his master's grave, Bum was beloved in his own times. The dog seems to have come to town as a stowaway on a steamer. He arrived at the peak of the boom—1886—and was befriended by a Chinese fisherman, Ah Wo Sue, who took care of him; and a journalist, James Edward Friend, who made his famous. Bum lost a leg in 1887, but that did not slow him down, as he visited regularly throughout the downtown area, and attended all concerts and parades. He also liked to travel, going to Coronado on the ferry and Los Angeles on the train. He is shown here in 1894 when he was injured by a horse. As he aged his rheumatism became severe and in 1898 the County board of Supervisors ordered him cared for at the County Hospital, where he stayed until he died. So fond of Bum was the community that his picture adorned dog licenses for years afterwards. Photograph courtesy San Diego Historical Society Public Library Collection

Water was always a problem in San Diego. At first there were wells and water carts, but if the town was going to amount to much, a larger, more dependable, and more convenient water supply would have to be secured. In the 1880s the first large steps in that direction were taken with the construction of a dam on Boulder Creek in the Cuyamaca Mountains, and a forty-five-mile flume to carry the water to town. The flume, shown here in 1889 in its finished state, had to go through eight tunnels and over 315 trestles before the water got to San Diego. The flume was never totally satisfactory and eventually was replaced, but a start on a dependable water supply had been made. Other major projects of the time were the Sweetwater Dam (when completed in 1888, the highest in the United States), and the Lower Otay Dam (finished in 1879 but destroyed in the flood of 1916). Photograph courtesy of the California State Library

Transportation was the key to the evolution of San Diego in this period. That meant the port and the transcontinental railroad for both commerce and movement of people into and out of the area. It also meant the development of local railroads to provide transportation in the immediate area. One of these smaller railroads was the Pacific Beach and La Jolla Railroad, shown here in 1888. Called "The dinky train that went to La Jolla" by Katherine Leng, she says it seemed to mostly carry school children. Other local lines included the Coronado Railroad, the National City and Otay, and the Cuyamaca and Eastern, all important in opening their respective areas to settlement. Photograph courtesy of The Bancroft Library, University of California, Berkeley

As agricultural development and transportation facilities grew in the 1880s, a number of rural towns were established east and north of San Diego: Ramona, Lakeside, San Marcos, and El Cajon, to name a few. El Cajon, whose main street as of 1887 is depicted here, was laid out by prominent San Diego merchant Ephraim W. Morse, and heavily promoted, with carriages taking prospective buyers to the beautiful El Cajon Valley to see the prospective settlement. Photograph courtesy of the California State Library

Whereas El Cajon was begun as an agricultural-commercial center, Del Mar was created as a beach resort town. The main developer was Col. Jacob Shell Taylor, a former scout for Buffalo Bill and the owner of Rancho Los Penasquitos. In 1882 he bought the site for the town and laid out streets and built hotels and other facilities. One of the main drawing cards was this swimming pool on the beach. It was constructed of sand, stone, and cement on the edge of the surf, and was filled with water from the sea tides. Its main advantage was that it kept the bathers safe from "the dreaded stingaree." Photograph courtesy of The Bancroft Library, University of California, Berkeley

Still another feature of the towns established near San Diego in this period is illustrated by this 1888 photograph of Encinitas (just north of Del Mar). Many of the new towns were built on the railroad line, which went from San Diego north to San Bernardino. It provided means of transportation and made the rural areas accessible for tourism, commerce, and agriculture. The importance of the railroad is emphasized in this photograph, in which the railroad station (far right of photograph) dominates the new community of Encinitas. Photograph courtesy of the California State Library

The most spectacular of the adjacent towns developed in the 1880s was Coronado. Originated by two speculators, E. S. Babcock and H. L. Story, and later acquired by John D. Spreckels, this settlement included a town, a streetcar system, ferryboats to connect it with San Diego—and most especially, the Hotel Del Coronado, regarded by many then and now as one of the most magnificent Victorian resort hotels in America. The hotel itself is shown in the first picture, just after its completion (it registered its first guests in February 1888). The other two photographs show some of the entertainments available to the vacationers at that time. One is the boathouse, an architectural jewel in itself. On the land behind the boathouse, a large tent city was set up in 1901, which included cabana-type dwellings, restaurants, and various forms of entertainments. It flourished until after the First World War. The other photograph shows people hunting (with the hotel faintly visible in the background). The entire peninsula was owned by the Babcock-Story interests and hunting was one of the frequently advertised activities the Hotel Del Coronado offered. Photographs courtesy of the Center for Regional History, San Diego State University; and The Bancroft Library, University of California, Berkeley

This picture says about all there is to say. In 1888 after several years of boom in which the population went from five thousand to forty thousand and real estate prices skyrocketed, it all came crashing down. By 1890, the population was only about sixteen thousand and real estate prices were depressed, bank deposits were down and it would take twenty years before San Diego would regain the population it had at the peak of the boom. In addition to the deflation of population and business, the bust brought plain old human misery. One witness said "there was actually suffering among those who had lost their little all, and were unable to raise money enough to get away." Because of the distress, burglary increased considerably and the number of people arrested and awaiting trial exceeded the capacity of the courts. Unless one could post bail, the wait in jail for trial in 1888 and 1889 was likely to be six months. As George Marston remembered it: "The boom and the collapse were tremendous." Photograph courtesy of the San Diego Historical Society—Ticor Collection

Although the bust had occurred when this street scene (looking south on Fifth from "G") was photographed in 1889, it was obvious much substantial was still left in San Diego. Solid, impressive Victorian brick buildings had replaced the mostly wooden frame buildings seen in the photographs at the beginning of this chapter. Public transportation, utilities and a more elaborate government were in place. Important educational, social and cultural foundations had been laid. San Diego was not dead; it was just going to rest for a decade or so. Photograph courtesy of the Center for Regional History, San Diego State University

Despite the Crash of 1888, San Diego was still a thriving small town, and its economic center was still its port. This 1890 photograph emphasizes that, with its view of the lumber yards (remember virtually the entire town has been built of imported lumber); the locomotive indicating the arrival—finally—of the railroad; and the ships in harbor, to remind us that the sea was still the major means of passenger and commercial transportation at this time. Photograph courtesy of the Center for Regional History, San Diego State University

4

A Period Of Quiet Consolidation

1890-1909

—

Between the Crash of 1888 and the beginning of the planning for the Panama-California Exposition in 1909, San Diego spent a quiet two decades firming up her foundations for future growth and providing a pleasant environment for her inhabitants. Population changed slowly, going from around 16,200 in 1890 to only 39,600 in the 1910 census. You were likely to hear comments like Marie Mayrhofer's: "It was a beautiful town when we came here in 1906."

There were a number of interesting events and activities to capture the town's attention during the period. The first visit by an in-office president of the United States occurred when President William Henry Harrison visited in 1891. The first of many Cabrillo Celebrations was staged in 1892. There was a bank crisis in 1906 which made some nervous. The United States Navy became increasingly important to the city, and provided excitement with the horrible tragedy on board the *Bennington* in 1905 and with the colorful visit of the Great White Fleet in 1908. The Navy also brought activity to the port during the Spanish-American War, which the city celebrated with patriotic fervor appropriate to the time. San Diego also did what it could in 1906 to help the victims of the San Francisco earthquake.

Some very basic cultural institutional foundations were also laid during this period. The point can be made easily simply by listing: a new state normal school (the precursor of San Diego State University), a new Carnegie library building, the Scripps Institution of Oceanography, the Amphion Society for encouragement of music, the Theosophical Institute at Point Loma with its various academic and artistic parts, and the Fisher Opera House which attracted major talent to the city. The most popular park of the area, Mission Cliffs Gardens, came into being, and work began toward making City Park (Balboa Park, in due time) one of the finest in the country.

In business and commerce, the city experienced fairly solid and steady— not boom—growth. Agricultural production in the county grew and became one of the mainstays of the economy. Much of the town was concerned with local businesses—wholesale, retail, and service. Major business enterprises— electric power, streetcars and ferries, and commercial properties—were developed by John Spreckels. Other enterprises were led by E. W. Scripps, Spreckels's most hated enemy.

The 1890-1910 period was one of transition and consolidation in a number of ways. For one thing, many prominent members of the original founding generation passed from the scene as Father Ubach, Alonzo Horton, E. W. Morse, and Matthew Sherman all died. Even the Horton House was torn down. A new generation of leaders for the first third of the twentieth century came to

the fore—John Spreckels, E. W. Scripps, George Marston, Ed Fletcher, Louis Wilde, Kate Sessions, Dr. Harry Wegeforth, and Dr. Charlotte Baker.

Several aspects of the city's basic infrastructure were improved from 1890 to 1909. Water was probably the biggest problem facing the city; up to this point wells, especially in Old Town and Mission Valley, were the main source of water. That clearly was not adequate and leaders like Ed Fletcher and Frank Kimball worked for the establishment of several dams—Cuyamaca, Otay, and Sweetwater—and distribution systems. Internal transportation was also developed. After Spreckels took over the system, the streetcar grid was improved and extended so that by 1909 it served virtually all settled areas of the town and was providing the impetus for growth outward. Previously begun local and regional railroads continued to provide service to far and nearly-far points like Lakeside, Otay, and La Jolla.

Some important developments occurred in politics and the political organization of the community. The structure of city government was changed and there developed a network of groups and committees which began to exert positive leadership. A typically Progressive era city charter change came in 1906 when the City Council was reduced from an unmanageable twenty-seven to nine. Although San Diego had not experienced the "machine" government and corruption which had characterized so many cities in turn-of-the-century America, its 1906 charter was one of the first in the country to include initiative, referendum, and recall.

Two examples of citizen leadership relate to the park and to the Nolen plan. The park developments were the work of a Park Improvement Committee set up in 1902; this was in keeping with the national "City Beautiful" trend and over twelve hundred similar committees throughout the United States. Among its activities, it hired the head of New York's Central Park, Samuel Parsons, to provide

If the years from 1867 to the 1880s could be called the "Age of Alonzo Horton," the years from 1888 to the 1920s could be called the "Age of John D. Spreckels." The wealthy sugar fortune heir came to San Diego on his yacht in 1887, saw the possibilities of the city and for decades afterward poured money and care into it. He remodeled the wharf, built the San Diego and Arizona Railroad, expanded water systems, built major buildings, the streetcar system, bailed out the Hotel Del Coronado, supported the 1915 Exposition, improved Balboa Park, bought the San Diego *Union* and *Tribune* newspapers—the list goes on and on. As one resident of the time, Alice Heyneman, put it: "This was a Spreckels town like a town is a company town." He "owned the City!" Photograph courtesy of the San Diego Historical Society—Ticor Collection

the first significant masterplan for Balboa Park. In many ways, it was crucial in shaping the future of the park with the emphasis on open space rather than buildings. The Chamber of Commerce had come into being earlier and had done much to publicize and promote the area, with the publication of booklets and other publicity materials. Under pressure from a leading merchant, George Marston, it also underwrote the hiring of nationally known architect and city planner, John Nolen, to design a plan for the development of the city. The plan, released to the public in 1909, was based on Nolen's assumption that "the scenery is varied and exquisitely beautiful" and it should be "looked upon as precious assets to be preserved and enhanced." His suggested plan involved grouping public buildings around a plaza, and development of a Bay Plaza which could confine the harbor to the southern part of the town, and keep the bayfront as open as possible for an elaborate park system. The drawings suggest plans that would have made San Diego one of the most spectacularly beautiful cities in the world. Unfortunately, no one paid much attention to Nolen's plan.

Thus the 1890-1909 period showed some slow growth, some ambitious plans and amazing foresight, and some failure to seize the opportunity and to take advantages of the city's natural assets. That same thing could *not* be said of the next decade, when this little city of less than forty thousand people pulled off a beautiful and successful international exposition which did much to set the style of the future city.

This 1899 scene on Broadway looking south from Second Street, gives a good overview of the town Spreckels dominated. It shows the growing number of substantial buildings and the loss of the frontier atmosphere which was present only a decade or so earlier. The photograph also shows one of the major developments within the town in this period—the streetcar system. An earlier horse-drawn trolley system had been established, but had not been too successful. In 1886 the San Diego Street Car Company was chartered and built an eight-and-a-half-mile system of rails. It, too, did not do well and in 1892 the San Diego Electric Railway Company (a Spreckels organization, naturally) took over and completed the streetcar system which served the city until 1949. Photograph courtesy of The Bancroft Library, University of California, Berkeley

When President William Henry Harrison visited San Diego on April 23, 1891, it marked the first time an in-office president of the United States had been to town. It was appropriate that the first presidential visit was by a Republican, because San Diego had become a strongly Republican town in the Horton era, and has remained one until the present. The city made much of Harrison's tour, giving him a parade around the city and a rally with an estimated five thousand in attendance. The president stayed at the Hotel Del Coronado, and is shown here descending the steps of that establishment. Photograph courtesy of the Center for Regional History, San Diego State University

Cabrillo Celebration S...

In 1892 a new event came to town, the Cabrillo Celebration. Suggested by the *Sun* to assist in bringing economic recovery after the Crash of 1888, it quickly grew into a lavish three-day event with a reenactment of Cabrillo's landing as the centerpiece. The event was advertised widely, especially in the West, including the exploding of bombs loaded with promotional literature several hundred feet over the heads of beachgoers on Redondo Beach. It was considered by one community leader of the time "one of the greatest advertisements San Diego ever had." It was so successful that it was repeated for some years, as indicated by this 1894 reenactment of Cabrillo's landing in the midst of the gaily decorated harbor. Photograph courtesy of The Bancroft Library, University of California, Berkeley

Between 1890 and 1910, fishing continued to be a major industry in San Diego. As the Chinese fishermen were squeezed out, other ethnic groups moved in. Some Italian and Japanese fishermen arrived in this period, but the dominant group was the Portuguese. As early as 1880 they comprised 17 percent of the fishermen in the bay. They fished in small boats for albacore, bonito, and yellowtail, both along the shore and up to one hundred miles out to sea. By 1897 they were numerous enough to organize the Portuguese Union Fish Company of La Playa. In the years that followed, they added boat design, construction and repair facilities, and in 1911, a cannery. With the Japanese, they laid the foundation for the modern tuna industry. In these two photographs, Portuguese fishermen are processing their catches in San Diego Bay. In the first, the fishermen are cleaning their catch; in the second they are selling tuna to fish dealers. Both pictures show the small boats they fished from. Photographs courtesy of the California Historical Society, San Francisco

Despite the arrival of rail connections via the Santa Fe system, San Diego remained very much a port city, and would for a long time. That is emphasized in this 1890 view of two large vessels tied up at the wharves, with the city in the background. Part of the reason was a spate of wharf building about this time. In 1888 Spreckels began a coal bunker wharf with a capacity of fifteen thousand tons of coal. Other wharfs were Russ Lumber Company, West Coast Lumber Company, Benson's Wharf, and Standard Oil's tanker wharf. As Jerry MacMullen reminds us in *They Came by Sea,* "While a veritable armada of tall ships headed for San Diego from Swansea and Wellington and Hamburg and both Newcastles, that man-made marvel, Los Angeles Harbor, still was on the drawing boards and San Diego was the seaport for most of Southern California." Photograph courtesy of the Center for Regional History, San Diego State University

When a streetcar or cable car company installed a line, it needed an attraction at the end to draw riders. This led to the establishment of one of San Diego's primary attractions, Mission Cliff Gardens, which flourished from 1889 to 1929. It was built on the cliffs overlooking Mission Valley and was landscaped with botanical gardens, a Japanese garden, aviary, deer paddock, and ostrich farm. There were theatrical performances, a beer garden, and a merry-go-round. As Elizabeth McPhail remembers it, "The Park was *the* place to go on Sunday afternoons." This view of the gardens was taken after the turn of the century, and shows the park with its foliage mature. The large building in the far background was the State Normal School, which had been erected in 1898. Photograph courtesy of the San Diego Historical Society—Ticor Collection

One of the main attractions of Mission Cliffs was the ostrich farm. As Beverly Potter has noted, it was actually operated by the Bentley Ostrich Farm and was not really in, but rather adjacent to, Mission Cliff Gardens. Potter quotes a child's reactions to the big birds: "Several times I . . . peeped through a dollar-sized knothole. Each time I encountered a big, rolling eye on the other side. Evidently the ostriches like to gaze at the outside world." Photograph courtesy of the California Historical Society, San Francisco

91

The ostrich farm was not there just for children to look at; it was there to provide ostrich feathers, which were the mainstay of ladies' elaborate hats in the period. As late as 1911, there was a large workshop adjacent to the Mission Cliff Gardens where workers processed the feathers for commercial use. Eventually the popularity of the automobile (most of which were open until the 1930s) ended the ostrich feather business by blowing away many ladies' feathered hats. Photograph courtesy of the San Diego Historical Society—Ticor Collection

Two things come together to hasten the reconstruction in 1909 of the Estudillo House, one of the earliest and most substantial Mexican period houses in Old Town. For one thing, for a number of years the romanticization of California's Hispanic past had been growing, and the Estudillo House played a part as "Ramona's Marriage Place" from Helen Hunt Jackson's novel, *Ramona.* As such, the house was a prime tourist attraction. At the same time, the Spreckels interests bought the railroad system in Old Town and needed an attraction at the end of the line to draw riders. Hence local architect Hazel Waterman was hired to direct the reconstruction of the house. She did extensive research into building materials and methods of the 1800s, and worked out construction specifications in extreme detail to guarantee quality reconstruction. She stressed everything had to be done the "old way" and even specified that the adobe bricks and tiles had "to be made by Mexicans only." As this picture of the construction of the corridor around the patio illustrates, her orders were followed. The construction techniques here are identical to those seen in the photograph of the model of the San Diego Mission on page 19. Photograph courtesy of the San Diego Historical Society Research Archives

Balboa Park had been set aside in 1868, but did not amount to much until a Park Improvement Committee was established and George Marston funded the hiring of internationally-known park designer and administrator Samuel Parsons to develop a master plan for the site. With that plan as a guide, and through the efforts of Kate Sessions and others who planted thousands of trees (such as the six thousand shown in this March 7, 1904 Arbor Day planting session), the park began its evolution into one of the nation's most beautiful. As the park's main historian, Greg Montes, has noted all of this was part of the nation's "City Beautiful" movement; by 1904 there were over twelve hundred local civic improvement committees in the nation. In developing its park, San Diego was in the national mainstream. Photograph courtesy of the San Diego Historical Society—Ticor Collection

The performing arts—and a racial discrimination court case—came to town with the opening of the Fisher Opera House on January 12, 1892. Costing $100,000, it was regarded as one of the finest opera houses on the coast. It hosted many theatrical performances and musical performances: *Pirates of Penzance*, Ignace Paderewski, John Philip Sousa's band, for instance. After the bank crash of 1906 it fell on hard times and was bought by Madame Tingley, who renamed it the "Isis." The Opera House was also the site of an incident which led to one of the nation's earliest civil rights court cases. In 1897 an Afro-American businessman and his wife, Edward and Mary Anderson, bought tickets to a performance; they were not allowed to sit in the seats they had purchased, but were told they could stand in the balcony with the other blacks. They sued and won $150 damages, although the case later was overturned on appeal. Photograph courtesy of the San Diego Historical Society—Ticor Collection

Further evidence of cultural growth of San Diego was the construction of an elegant new library building. A public library had been organized in 1882 but by the 1890s it desperately needed better quarters. Under the aggressive leadership of Alonzo Horton's young wife, Lydia Knapp Horton, the city obtained a gift of sixty thousand dollars for a library building from Andrew Carnegie. It was the first Carnegie library funded west of the Mississippi. Following incredible bickering over just about everything involved in the project, the city finally built the library, which was dedicated on April 23, 1902. The landscaping was done by Kate Sessions and paid for by George Marston. Photograph courtesy of the San Diego Historical Society—Ticor Collection

San Diego was also growing educationally. In 1897 the state authorized the establishment of a normal school in San Diego, and it opened its doors at a temporary site in the fall of 1898. This photograph shows the building (at Sixth and "F"); the first class of students is clearly visible in the windows of the third floor and the class dog awaits curbside. Within a year the state Normal School moved to a classical-style building on Park Avenue. In time it moved to Montezuma Mesa and eventually became San Diego State University, with over thirty-three thousand students. Photograph courtesy of the San Diego State University Archives

Some extraordinary women lived in San Diego at the turn of the century—Kate Sessions, Lydia Knapp Horton, Dr. Charlotte Baker, and especially Ellen Browning Scripps. The sister of newspaperman E. W. Scripps, she came to the city with her brother and lived in La Jolla from 1897 until her death at age 96 in 1932. Although extremely shy, Scripps supported many causes in the city—the Bishop's School, the Torrey Pines Preserve, the Children's Playground in La Jolla, the La Jolla Women's Club, San Diego State University, the Zoological Society, and especially the Scripps Institution of Oceanography, which was established in La Jolla in a small shack, but later removed to its permanent site as the result of gifts by Ellen Browning Scripps. It is the oldest, largest, and perhaps the most prestigious institution of oceanography in the United States. Photograph courtesy of the Center for Regional History, San Diego State University

As San Diego began to grow, public services were introduced. A city police department was set up in 1889. Jefferson Keno Wilson was its chief from 1909 to 1917, and was the best-known early lawman in the city. Wilson began his career in Oceanside as a deputy sheriff, worked for the United States Customs service and joined the San Diego police as a patrolman on December 18, 1899. He was soon promoted to a mounted patrolman (shown here at age 38, about 1900), and finally to chief of police. As chief, he presided over the police during its efforts to eradicate the red light district, and during the I.W.W. Riots of 1912. Photograph courtesy of the San Diego Historical Society—Ticor Collection

J. KENO. WILSON

This 1898 photograph of Sixth Street with the utility poles marching off into the distance shows the growing impact of electricity on the little city. Whatever the advantages may have been in convenience, they did not extend to aesthetics. Electricity had come to town in 1886 with the Jenny Electrick Company of Indianapolis, which was bought out by the San Diego Fuel and Electric Light Company in 1887. By the mid-1890s, electricity had been extended over eight miles out from the center of the city. Photograph courtesy of the San Diego Historical Society—Ticor Collection

San Diego has never been particularly hospitable to organized labor, but labor unions have existed since the 1800s, when various craft unions—typographical, cigar makers, bakers, longshoremen, sailors, fishermen, and drovers—began to organize. One such group was the Team Drivers' Union, assembled here for a parade in 1900. All the groups were affiliated with a San Diego Federated Trades and Labor Council (1891) and eventually the national American Federation of Labor (although relations with the AFL were rocky during most of this period). The local unions scored some victories on work hours and pay issues, but were always defeated on political matters. Photograph courtesy of the Center for Regional History, San Diego State University

Several utopian colonies were established in San Diego during this period. One was the Little Landers Colony set up in San Ysidro in 1909, but the largest was the School for the Revival of Lost Mysteries of Antiquities set up by Madam Katherine A. Tingley and the Theosophical Society on Point Loma. The establishment, shown here being dedicated on February 23,

1897, operated until 1942 and drew followers from all over the world. The school was supposed to be "a temple of living light, lighting up the dark places of the earth," and had as its centerpiece a boarding-school system for children and adults. Its program was heavily oriented toward

culture and is fondly remembered by many graduates, although some others likened their experiences there to a concentration camp. The site is now occupied by Point Loma Nazarene College. Photograph courtesy of The Bancroft Library, University of California, Berkeley

While the city sent down deep roots in the 1890s and 1900s, the rural areas continued to grow as well. After the 1890s increased transportation facilities improved marketing and new crops—especially citrus fruits—were introduced in large quantities. This "ranch" surrounded by young orchards is typical of many of the rural establishments at this period. Photograph courtesy of the Center for Regional History, San Diego State University

Although railroads were beginning to penetrate much of the San Diego Backcountry, stagecoaches continued to operate. For example, to get to Julian or Warner Springs it was still necessary to take the stage. The niece of one of the stage operators, Katherine N. Leng, described the process as this: "You took the train to Foster, where you caught the stage, which left about 10 A.M. and arrived in Julian about 8 P.M." The stages were Concords and carried passengers, mail and the Wells Fargo express. They were "miserable things to ride in. The motion made the passengers sea-sick and the dust was terrible. If the curtains were drawn, it made the coach very stuffy." This 1905 photograph shows the stage at the depot in Foster, loaded and ready to depart for Julian. Photograph courtesy of the San Diego Historical Society—Ticor Collection

As the Backcountry developed, San Diego served as its trading center. An example would be the activities of Klauber and Levi, Wholesale Grocers (founded in 1869 as Steiner and Klauber). Their salesman, Clarence A. Henderson, shown in 1891 in his buggy in front of a rural store, travelled the north county towns of Oceanside, Fallbrook, Escondido, Temecula, Elsinore, Perris, Hemet, and Valley Center. He would send out his card prior to his visit. Photograph courtesy of the Klauber Wangenheim Company

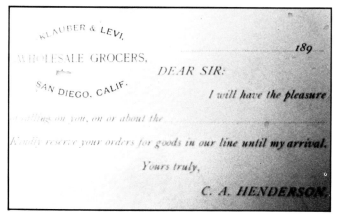

Another way the rural areas supported San Diego was by supplying agricultural goods for processing in the city. Melville Klauber remembers working in a flour mill around Twelfth and "K" streets, milling wheat brought in from Bear Valley, El Cajon, Escondido, and other points in wagons like this one, shown in 1898. As Klauber put it, "San Diego was quite a wheat producing country." Photograph courtesy of the Klauber Wangenheim Company

The treatment of Native Americans in San Diego paralleled the national pattern—racial discrimination which led to exclusion from the mainstream of life. By the 1870s most Indians in San Diego were displaced from town and pushed out to rural areas, and often onto reservations. The first reservations had been established in 1876 and by 1910 there were sixteen reservations in San Diego County (with two more added in 1931).

Most of the Indians were Cahuilla, Cupeño, and Kumeyaay. This Isaiah West Taber photograph of an Indian *rancheria* near San Diego shows that until around 1900 some Native Americans lived on the edge of town, where they served as a useful source of labor for the white majority. Photograph courtesy of The Bancroft Library, University of California, Berkeley

The earliest Afro-Americans in San Diego tended to live in the rural areas; after 1890 they responded to increased job opportunities and began to move into town. Although never very large in terms of percentage of the population, black Americans still constituted a significant community in San Diego after 1890. They ran businesses, and were active in churches, and social and professional organizations. The black community was large enough to have social stratification in it; for instance the Violet Club was for elite women only. This photograph of two girls and a dog, taken in 1895 by Charles Klindt of the Chicago Gallery, shows the degree of prosperity some Afro-Americans had attained at this time. Photograph courtesy of the San Diego Historical Society—Ticor Collection

While many Afro-Americans were laborers or unskilled employees of one kind or the other, others owned their own business. An example would be the I.X.L. Laundry on Tenth and Island, shown here in an 1890s snapshot. Although the man to the left is unidentified, the others in the picture are Mrs. Parker, Mame (or Mary) Anderson, and Edward Anderson, the owner. Other businesses owned by blacks at the time were grocery stores, several junk and second-hand stores, and a watch shop. Photograph courtesy of the San Diego Historical Society—Ticor Collection

In this period, Fort Rosecrans on Point Loma became a United States Army installation. The Army began with the installation of some defensive batteries, and then the government built a quarantine station and coaling station at Ballast Point. Not until 1898 were troops stationed there regularly; they were the Battery D, Third Artillery, moved over from the San Diego barracks. From this point to 1959 when the area was transferred to the United States Navy, Fort Rosecrans was a major part of the port defenses for the city. This postcard is somewhat fanciful in that the ships in the harbor are obviously painted in. It is possible they are meant to depict the Great White Fleet of 1908. Photograph courtesy of the California State Library

In the years afters its permanent occupation by troops, Fort Rosecrans was considered a "highly desirable" duty station, and many applied for transfer there, or sought to re-enlist in order to stay there. Some in the army jokingly called it an "old soldiers' home," and many men stationed there remained in the city and some became prominent citizens. It would appear that card playing (surely not illegal gambling) was a part of life in the "old soldiers' home." Photograph courtesy of the Cabrillo National Monument

One of San Diego's most shocking disasters came in 1905 as the U.S.S. *Bennington* blew up. The old patrol gunboat, which had been in and out of San Diego since 1897, was preparing to sail on July 21, 1905, when, at 10:38 A.M., an explosion sent superheated steam throughout the ship. Sixty-five people died as a result of the disaster, most from the boiling steam. After the explosion, ships in the harbor rushed to the rescue, including even the Coronado ferryboat. Civilians manned hospitals and did what they could for the injured. The stunned city gathered on July 23 at Fort Rosecrans as forty-seven of the bodies were laid to rest in a mass grave. To commemorate their memory, a large monument was raised at the site. These photographs show the massive damages on the deck of the *Bennington*, and the memorial services at Fort Rosecrans. Both photographs courtesy of the Maritime Museum of San Diego

The 1908 visit of Teddy Roosevelt's Great White Fleet to San Diego was one of the most exciting events of the period. The fleet came to town on April 14, with the battleships anchoring offshore and the smaller vessels coming into the harbor. On April 15 the city threw a huge celebration with bonfires and banners. Fifty thousand citizens (more than the population of the town) turned out to watch a parade of five thousand seamen on Broadway. Marston Burnham remembers: "Yes, it was a tremendous sight." One historian noted that while residents invited the men to their own table for meals, "the Stingaree District had out the red carpet as well as the red lights." It was believed that the visit did much to publicize San Diego. Photograph courtesy of the UCLA Special Collections

The Matt F. Heller family was prominent in the 1890s and after. Their grocery store was on the way to becoming a San Diego institution. In time they had forty-two stores, before selling out to what eventually became the Safeway chain. During the 1890s the family lived in a solid Victorian-style house at Eleventh and "F" Street. The family picture shown here illustrates several things about San Diego at the time—the predominance of Victorian architectural styles (despite the fact that the wood to build them had to be imported a thousand miles); the absence of lawns in the era before abundant water; and the unpaved streets and lack of concrete sidewalks, which occasioned many complaints about the dust and/or mud. Photograph courtesy of the San Diego Historical Society—Ticor Collection

By the turn of the century, there was a sizable German population in San Diego. One of the institutions they created was a local chapter of the German-based cultural and athletic fraternity, the Turnverein. First organized in 1885, but reorganized as the Concordia Turnverein in 1890, the organization was especially important on the local athletic and physical culture scene. They created the first gymnasium in the city and were responsible for introducing physical culture into the public schools. Many citizens from the early half of the twentieth century remember being introduced to gymnastics, acrobatics, and other sports by the Turners. As indicated by their seal, they stressed "Sound Mind/Sound Body." The opening page of their recordbook indicates their early origins in San Diego. Photograph courtesy of the San Diego Historical Society Research Archives

The Gay Nineties were not called "gay" for nothing; saloons abounded in the city. One of the most substantial was that of Till A. Burnes at the corner of Fifth and "E" streets, the "finest fitted up saloon in town." This was, according to Ad Pearson, *the saloon of San Diego* and replaced an earlier establishment which Burnes had filled with various animals kept in cages or chained outside, plus a large number of monkeys who ran free inside the bar. It is not surprising that a chapter of the Women's Christian Temperance Union was formed in San Diego in 1884. Photograph courtesy of the San Diego Historical Society—Ticor Collection

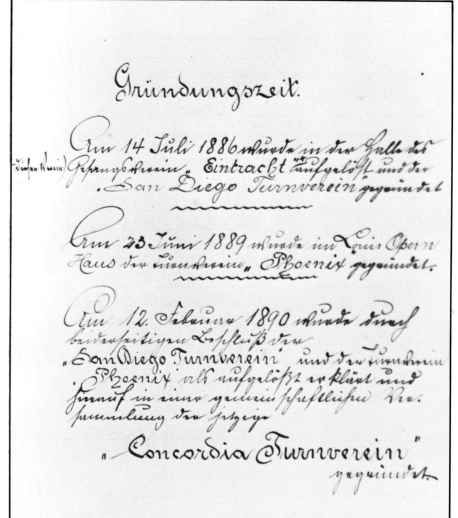

Competitive sports were popular in school—and were not restricted to men! There was, as shown here in 1900, a girls' basketball team at Russ High School. It is hard to imagine them moving in the heavy clothing, but obviously they did, and with vigor. The team was identified only as: Storey (center); Dodge (left guard); Bagby (left forward); Halstead (near forward); Myars (right guard); and Anderson, Jones, Davis and Wilicarp (substitutes). The high school principal at the time was Harry Halliday. Photograph courtesy of the San Diego High School Alumni Association

The athletic activities of Russ High School also included a football team. The 1891-92 edition is shown in their version of a very macho pose. The team members are identified as (left to right) Jacoby, Brimhall, R. Peck, Judson, Otis, Bainer, Crosby, Hamlin, Watson, Pendergest, and H. Halzard. Photograph courtesy of the San Diego Historical Alumni Association

As San Diego settled down to a period of steady turn-of-the-century life, the high school played an important role as a cultural, social, and sporting center. Some of the social life can be seen in this snapshot of pupils eating sack lunches at the rainwater cistern on the northeast corner of Russ High School. They supplemented lunch with cistern water drunk from the common tin cup. The student on the right is E. Johnson (later Mrs. M. W. Neuman) who provided the photograph. Photograph courtesy of the San Diego High School Alumni Association

Departure of Co. B 7th Infantry N.G.C. San Diego. May 5th 1898. Slocum Pho[to]

On May 5, 1898, Company B of the California National Guard departed for war, with the farewell of hundreds of citizens urging them on. They were going to fight in the relatively minor conflict which Teddy Roosevelt called "A Splendid Little War" and which produced more casualties from disease than from battle. In addition to the departing army, the war brought increased navy activity to the harbor. Photograph courtesy of the San Diego Historical Society—Ticor Collection

Because of a number of navigational problems, the 1855 lighthouse on Point Loma was replaced by a more modern one at water's edge in 1891. As years went by the old lighthouse (erroneously called the Old Spanish Lighthouse in the era of romanticization of the California past), fell into disrepair. It became, however, a favorite spot for a Sunday picnic, previewing its future role as the centerpiece of the Cabrillo National Monument. This is an 1893 picnic of Mr. Field and Miss Grove (the social secretary at the Hotel Del Coronado) and guest. Photograph courtesy of the California Historical Society, San Francisco

Outings to the beaches and waterfront cliffs were also important activities at the turn of the century. One of the most popular areas was La Jolla, with its spectacular cliffs and even a cave. This photograph shows a family gathering near the caves in 1909. It is a rather typical photograph of the time, showing a carefully (even artfully) posed collection of people against a spectacular natural backdrop. Photograph courtesy of The Bancroft Library, University of California, Berkeley

With its waterfront location, San Diego has long been heavily involved in water sports. As early as 1850 soldiers at the barracks had organized a yacht club and races. In 1888 one of the longest running attractions came into being, the San Diego Rowing Club. Along with providing the scene for a large variety of activities and a meeting place for many of the city's most prominent citizens, the club has since 1892 sponsored a New Year's Day swim. The photograph shows the 1904 occasion. The objective is to prove "that swimming can be as much enjoyed in winter as in summer," and was designed to help publicize the mild climate of San Diego. Photograph courtesy of the San Diego Historical Society Public Library Collection

By the turn of the century, tourism was important to San Diego—and already a visit to Tijuana was a part of that scene. Several companies ran excursions to the town, which, gathering from the English language store signs, was quite ready to exploit the tourism. This 1905 photograph shows American tourists on the main street of Tijuana, posed in their serapes and Mexican hats, which they have undoubtedly just purchased. Photograph courtesy of The Bancroft Library, University of California, Berkeley

Sport fishing and ocean excursions were also becoming part of the tourist scene in San Diego. This 1900 photograph shows a group of tourists returning on the *Golden West* from an excursion to the Coronado Islands. The photograph is an "Arcade View," meaning it was one of thousands of mounted photographs which were widely distributed throughout the country. They were a form of advertising the charms of the city, as well as a sort of geography lesson. Photograph courtesy of the Maritime Museum of San Diego

The twentieth century brought to San Diego the new contraption, the automobile. It is not clear who owned the first, but A. G. Spaulding (sporting goods magnate who came to San Diego as part of Madame Tingley's entourage) is one candidate. He is shown here with his wife in an automobile, probably on Point Loma. Although the automobile would be of more concern later, it did stir up some attention prior to 1910. For instance, there was a splendid race at Lakeside in 1907 in which Barney

Oldfield set a world speed record of sixty-five miles per hour. Photograph courtesy of the San Diego Historical Society—Ticor Collection

Unpaved streets had been the source of consternation since the town began—and the problem became more serious after the automobiles arrived. Finally, bond issues were passed in 1907 and 1909 and a number of streets were paved, mostly in the central portion of town. Jeanne Rimmer remembers that as late as the 1920s the streets were still so bad when it rained that you had to put "a big package of newspapers" down in front of you to walk on. "That is what you did. Because if you didn't, at every step you would pick up another inch of gunk." It would not appear, however, that these boys were too unhappy with the situation! Photograph courtesy of the San Diego Historical Society Public Library Collection

Ed Fletcher, George Marston, and John Nolen—three men who played a large part in the shaping of San Diego—are seen in 1908. Ed Fletcher arrived in San Diego at age fifteen and became one of the city's major real estate, water, and highway developers. George Marston came to San Diego in 1870 and worked in the mercantile business, eventually creating the city's first major department store. No one in its over two-hundred-year history spent more on making San Diego a better place than George Marston. He was a founder of the Normal School, backer of Balboa Park, the Exposition of 1915, Presidio Park, builder of Serra Museum, and much more. The third man, John Nolen, was hired by the Chamber of Commerce (mostly through Marston) to develop a plan for the city's development. He was one of the most prominent city planners and architects in the nation and it was impressive that a little city like San Diego would seek his services. Photograph courtesy of the San Diego Historical Society—Ticor Collection

Ever since Alonzo Horton put in a little garden across from Horton House, that site has been more-or-less the center of San Diego. It only became a city park, however, in 1890 and it did not take on its present character until 1910 when developer/politician Louis J. Wilde commissioned San Diego's most distinguished architect, Irving Gill, to design a fountain for the place. (Inasmuch as Wilde had taken over the U.S. Grant Hotel directly across the street from the plaza, it is likely his motivation was not entirely philanthropical). Gill designed a fountain in Grecian classic form, with moving water, lighting at night, and portraits of Cabrillo, Serra, and Horton. Shown here in a rare 1910 night photograph, this fountain has been the centerpiece of Horton Plaza ever since. Photograph courtesy of the San Diego Historical Society—Ticor Collection

new Dredger.

San Diego needed harbor improvements to become the major city it is today. Although San Diego Bay is a magnificent land-locked harbor, it was shallow and suffered silting problems. In time the San Diego River was rerouted from San Diego Bay into nearby False Bay, in order to stop the flow of silt into the harbor. A jetty was built at the entrance of the harbor to create a scouring effect in order to keep the entry clear. In addition, dredging was begun in 1891 and has continued to the present. The largest dredging program was begun in 1911 to prepare the harbor to receive the expected commercial and naval boom created by the opening of the Panama Canal. As the harbor was dredged for channels, the silt was used as fill to extend the shoreline considerably. By the end of the Second World War almost seventeen hundred acres of filled land had been created, and many major installations—the Naval Training Station, Marine Corps Recruit Depot, Lindbergh Field, the Embarcadero-Harbor Drive, and much of the aircraft industry, for example—had been built on that fill. This 1913 photograph shows the dredger deepening the harbor and piping the sludge to the tidelands behind the sea wall. Photograph courtesy of the San Diego Historical Society—Ticor Collection

Diego Cal. 8-14-13   2246

5

The City Takes Off

1910-1919

—

The second decade of the century saw a tremendous amount of activity and growth in the little city. The growth in numbers was impressive, as the population went from about forty thousand to nearly seventy-five thousand. The growth in other ways was truly spectacular. San Diego put together a highly praised Panama California Exposition; it saw revolution and disorder at home and across the border. San Diego lived through one of the largest floods in its history; and World War I, which did much to firm up the town's growing reputation as a "Navy Town." There was continual commercial growth with harbor improvements and changes, some due to the opening of the Panama Canal. Cultural and social institutions continued to prosper and one of the great zoos of the world had its inception in the 1910s.

Among the more fundamental developments, nothing was so basic as the Panama California Exposition of 1915 and 1916. It began to be discussed in 1909, mostly as a means to get the town moving again after the doldrums of the Great Crash of 1888 and the Bank Crisis of 1906. The idea was to use the opening of the Panama Canal to draw attention to San Diego and its attractions for commerce, tourism, agriculture, and quality of life. Much of the town's energy from 1870 on had been devoted to boosterism; as such it is a very typical western American city. Of those boosterism projects, none was more ambitious and certainly none had more permanent impact than the Exposition.

The Exposition was built with over a million dollars each of private and public money, and before it closed three million people had been through its gates. Because it was not allowed to compete with San Francisco's certified world exposition and because it began late, the fair did not attract many international or state exhibits. Thus it focused on San Diego and the West Coast, making it even more of a boosteristic (if there is such a word) enterprise than usual. It showed the world about San Diego mining, culture, agriculture, products, as well as showing the visitors a good time. From all accounts of the time, it seems that the most important thing it showed the people was San Diego. They came to the Panama California Exposition, but they talked about San Diego. One of the reasons was the beautiful Prado area of Balboa Park which had been surrounded—on a small walkable scale to create a village atmosphere—by baroque Spanish Colonial buildings. Coupled with the Mission Revival Santa Fe station which greeted most visitors on their arrival, a Hispanic tone was set. With the climate, the beauty of the natural setting, and the literally millions of plantings especially made for the Exposition, the city sparkled.

Of similar importance to San Diego was the effect of World War I on the

community. During that war both the Army and Navy began to understand fully the importance of the good climate for military purposes. Military aviation in San Diego had begun as early as 1911 and by the end of the war, San Diego was the site of the nation's first Army air base and had been the site of many U.S. Navy air firsts. A large Army Camp, Camp Kearny, serviced forty thousand men in the war. The United States Navy had already begun to move into the city in force before World War I, but the war accelerated that development. With the Navy at North Island, Camp Howard (later Marine Corps Recruit Depot), Naval Training Station, in temporary quarters at Balboa Park, and on ships stationed in the bay, San Diego became a veritable military armed camp. From this point, San Diego has always had a strong military flavor and a strong military element in the economy; as late as the 1950s, over 70 percent of the income in the area still came, directly or indirectly, from the military.

In this busy decade other things came to the little city on the bay. The direct rail connection to Yuma was completed in 1919 and on December 1, 1919, the first train left San Diego for Yuma on the San Diego and Arizona Railroad. It had been dreamed of since the 1840s, and was pushed to completion by John Spreckels with a little help by the United States government who saw its military potential and thus exempted it from wartime building restrictions.

As the automobile became more and more important, the significance of getting San Diego attached to the national highway network was as important as the nineteenth-century efforts to get the city tied to the railroad system. San Diego was much more successful with highways than it had been with railroads, and Ed Fletcher was the man most responsible.

Otherwise the economy and society of the city continued to develop much as it had before. Fishing remained

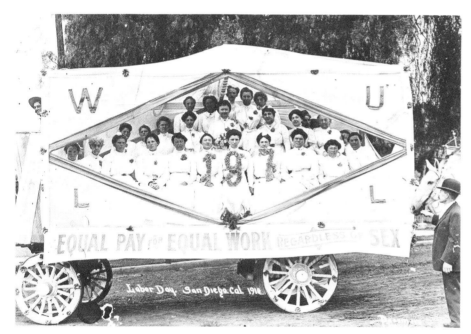

This 1912 photograph of San Diego Bay shows how the city was developing. Larger buildings are beginning to appear on the skyline. The obvious appearance of the Hotel Del Coronado, the piers and ships remind us that tourism and commerce were still major foundations of the city's economy at that point. Photograph courtesy of the Center for Regional History, San Diego State University

While San Diego was growing and prospering, it must be remembered that American women were working for improvements in their conditions. Floats by various women's groups were a normal feature in local parades. This particular one is by the Women's Union Label League No. 197 for the 1910 Labor Day parade. Its slogan, "Equal Pay for Equal Work Regardless of Sex," harkens back to the 1848 Seneca Falls Declaration and forward to the present. Photograph courtesy of the San Diego Historical Society—Ticor Collection

important, and Japanese fishermen came to dominate. Agriculture continued to grow, and harbor and port facilities continued to be improved and expanded. The film industry flirted with San Diego for awhile, before finally turning to Hollywood. There continued to be an interest in real cultural matters. For example, when the Amphion Club obtained use of the Spreckels Theatre in 1919 for their concerts, members lined up at 4:00 A.M. the first day in order to get seats; by 5:00 P.M. the next day the entire theatre had been subscribed, and many were turned away. In architecture the young designer Irving Gill was becoming more important as he developed his sparse style (with feints toward Craftsman and Mission Revival), which many see as a precursor of "modern" architectural styles. Spanish and Mission Revival styles came to dominate and give the city a special identity. Donal Hord had arrived in town to develop a distinctive style of sculpture which seems very "at home" in San Diego. There was also a growing concern for the city's historical past, although that would become more important in the next decade.

Aside from these fundamental developments some interesting events also occurred. San Diego was fascinated (and sometimes a little scared) by Mexico's revolution which began in 1910 and came close to home with a major battle in Tijuana in 1911. That in turn was the foundation for the Free Speech Movement of 1912, in which the Industrial Workers of the World, (I.W.W.) and other radical groups came into conflict with the conservative city. Those same conservatives also tried mightily to clean up the red-light district near downtown. Although they thought they did, the fact that most of the women arrested bought round-trip tickets when they left leads one to doubt the full extent of the Purity League's success in the Stingaree raid.

The city also suffered through the worst flood in its history. One dam was washed away and another partially washed out; Mission Valley filled from one side to the other. Unfortunately the city had hired a well-known rainmaker, Charles Hatfield, and he thought he caused the rain and demanded to be paid. The city refused and the courts basically sided with the city by saying that God, not Hatfield, had caused the rains.

The city also participated in its most famous mayoralty election, the "Geraniums vs. Smokestacks" fight of 1917. George Marston, who stood for quality of life and controlled growth, was one candidate; Louis Wilde, a recently arrived financier and banker and typical Southern California promoter, stood for heavy industrialism and as much growth as possible. After a very vigorous campaign, Wilde won. Fortunately he was not successful in attracting smokestacks to the city and thus the quality of life that made it so unique and attractive was preserved, at least for awhile longer. As Neil Morgan has pointed out in his *The Unconventional City*, San Diego's failures have basically made the city what it is.

Thus when the year 1919 came to a close, San Diego could look back to its busiest and its most successful decade. The city came out of it with a pride and a self-confidence that would carry it through the twenties, and even help it survive the Depression better than most places. San Diego was finally on the road toward becoming "America's Finest City."

Hardly had San Diego entered into the decade before the town was shaken by the Mexican Revolution against Porforio Diaz. The Revolution began in 1910, and in 1911, there were battles in Tijuana. American crowds gathered at the border to watch. These people are at the Customs House at the United States side of the border crossing. Photograph courtesy of the San Diego Historical Society—Ticor Collection

Americans were affected by the Mexican Revolution in several ways. One included the seizure by rebels of the San Diego and Arizona Railroad's locomotive No. 50 on May 9, 1911. Don Armstrong, the conductor, and others were taken prisoner, but all were released unharmed when the rebels were through with the train. Photograph courtesy of the San Diego Historical Society—Ticor Collection

The Mexican Revolution caused alarm in the United States and a variety of American armed units were sent to border areas. In San Diego troops were stationed at various points along the border. The Navy was also strengthened, as indicated by the disembarkation here on May 30, 1911, of this contingent of sailors. Photograph courtesy of the California Historical Society Library, San Francisco

A complicated event of the period, and one related to the Mexican turmoil, was the "Free Speech" controversy of 1912. The Industrial Workers of the World, a radical labor union, supported rebel elements of the Mexican Revolution. They, along with some socialists and Mexican revolutionaries, began to speak on the streets of San Diego—especially at the corner of Fifth and "E"—in support of their cause. Their rhetoric and small acts of vandalism upset the city and on January 8, 1912, the City Council passed an ordinance prohibiting speeches in a six-square-block area. A California Free Speech League chapter was organized, rallies followed and clashes occurred on February 8 and 10, culminating in a major conflict on April 5. Fire hoses

were used by the city to maintain order, and the combination of that action and the work of vigilantes effectively broke the riots by the middle of 1912. Photograph courtesy of the San Diego Historical Society— Ticor Collection

The Free Speech Riots brought one of America's most notable radicals, Emma Goldman, to town for one of her three visits to San Diego. She was secured by the police ("for her own safety"), and escorted onto the Los Angeles train. This May 21, 1912 photograph shows her (with back to the camera) at the jailhouse. Although Goldman got out of town without harm, the same cannot be said for her travelling companion, Ben Reitman, who was seized by vigilantes, taken to Linda Vista Mesa, stripped naked and had "I.W.W." branded on his buttocks with cigarettes. He was then covered with tar and, in absence of feathers, dusted with sagebrush. Brutality to demonstrators occurred many times during the ordeal; none of the vigilantes were ever indicted or tried for their

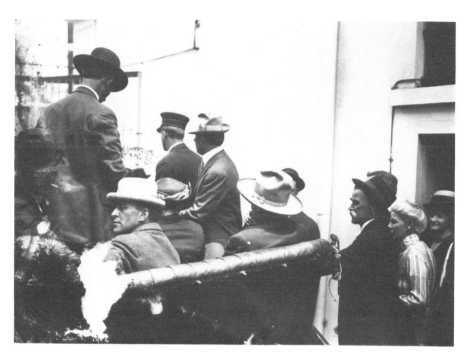

behavior, although the governor did send the state attorney general to San Diego for that purpose. Photograph courtesy of the San Diego Historical Society—Ticor Collection

If the Battle of Tijuana and the I.W.W. Riots were not enough, San Diego decided to launch a major attack on the red-light district in 1912. It was located in the area called the Stingaree, which included Chinatown, saloons, gambling establishments and female-companionship-for-hire. Mostly located between "H" and "K" streets between First and Fifth, it also included the City Hall! Katherine Leng described what she saw on a visit to the area: "There wasn't really much to see. Just long rows of buildings—I think they called them 'cribs'—and a door and window for each and the girls in their finery out in front. As we were walking along I heard somebody say 'Hello, Kate,' and there was a girl I had gone to school with! It was a long time before I was allowed to forget my buddy in the Stingaree!" Photograph courtesy of the San Diego Historical Society—Ticor Collection

The Stingaree was raided on November 10, 1912. The raids came as a result of the Purity League led by several ministers and a doctor, Charlotte Baker. In the best traditions of the Progressive period, they were concerned with both moral, and health and sanitation issues. The raid resulted in the arrest of 138 women, with most charged with vagrancy. They were fined, but their sentences were suspended if they would be on the three o'clock train that same day. Most went to Los Angeles, and observers noted many buying round-trip tickets. It is interesting that only two women agreed to reform. The red-light district was never the same again and in May of 1913, sailors on several Navy ships voted by a margin of 797 to 17 to take their liberty in San Francisco instead of San Diego (which had been most popular in previous years). Photograph courtesy of the San Diego Historical Society—Ticor Collection

"Auction Sale"
THE "Passing" of THE FIRE HORSE.
Modern Fire Fighting Apparatus
Forceing Them Out.
San Diego Cal. Progression.
Passmore Photo. 3-8-13

An indication of the growing importance of the automobile at this time is this March 8, 1913 auction of horses by the fire department. The new horseless fire engines had made their horses obsolete! Photograph courtesy of the San Diego Historical Society—Ticor Collection

An example of the new non-horse fire engines was this New Seagrave Fire Truck which had been purchased by the National City Fire Department in 1912. Here the department is shown after responding to a fire on Eighteenth Street at the Italian National Macaroni Factory which exploded and burned. Photograph courtesy of The Bancroft Library, University of California, Berkeley

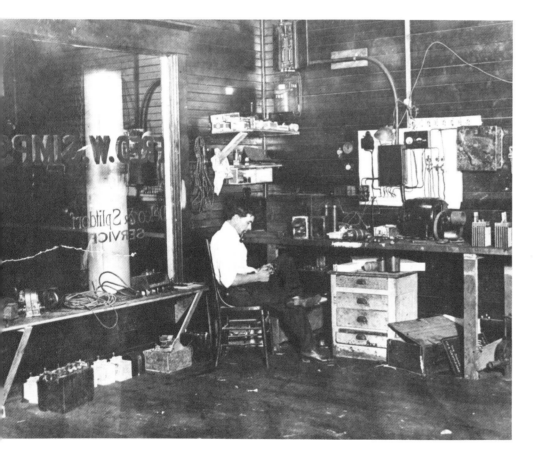

The automobile was clearly here to stay. In fact, one brand of car, the "Hunt" was even manufactured in Chula Vista in 1910, the only make of car ever built in San Diego County. The city's first auto dealership, Clyde and Arms Company, came into being, and the number of automobiles on the road now warranted repair shops. This one is Carlson and Simpson at Sixth and "A" streets in February of 1916. Inside the shop is Fred W. Simpson, who was also a city councilman. Photograph courtesy of the San Diego Historical Society— Ticor Collection

With the automobile capturing America, San Diego now had the same problem they had had when the railroad appeared—how do you get tied into the rest of the nation? San Diego worked diligently—with Ed Fletcher in the lead—to promote a link between San Diego and the new national highway system. To make an effective case, San Diego had to conquer two major impediments—the mountains and the shifting sands in Imperial County. Both were done (to some extent) in this period. A twelve-foot wide road was built up Mountains Springs Grade (which dropped one thousand feet in three miles) and its completion was celebrated with a big affair on April 10, 1913, when a large caravan of cars carrying eight hundred people converged on the site for speeches and celebrations. Photograph courtesy of the San Diego Historical Society—Ticor Collection

The other big problem with building a highway to the east was the stretch of sand dunes between San Diego and the Colorado River. Unless conquered, they required a 46-mile detour, which made it hard to sell San Diego (as opposed to hated Los Angeles) as part of the national highway system. It was conquered with a wooden road. First a flimsy two-track road was set down across six miles of sand; after 1915 a much more substantial wooden road (shown here) was laid down, with Ed Fletcher buying the lumber. The state then approved of the route, which helped considerably San Diego's case for designation as part of a national highway route. Photograph courtesy of the San Diego Historical Society—Ticor Collection

This poster heralds the Panama California Exposition held in San Diego in 1915 and 1916. It changed the city forever. The Exposition was designed to advertise the city at the time of the completion of the Panama Canal, and was built around the expectation that San Diego would be a major port of call for canal commerce. The Exposition was built with both private funds and a city bond issue. It was placed in Balboa Park (formerly called City Park), which would never be the same again. Photograph courtesy of the California State Library

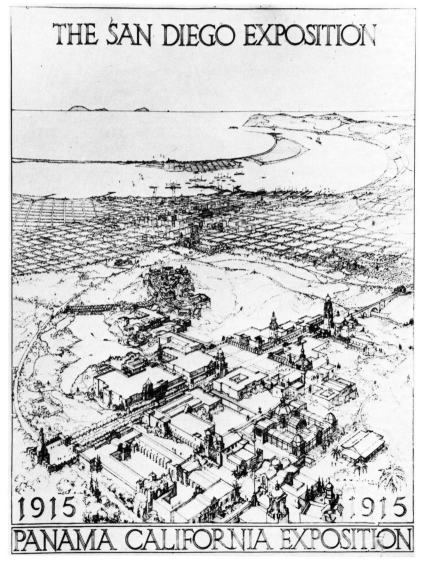

One of the key decisions had been to hire Bertram Grosvenor Goodhue to design the buildings; he developed a collection of buildings in the style of Hispanic colonial architecture, as illustrated by the magnificent California Tower and the Prado area, seen here in 1915 after the Panama California Exposition opened. The buildings in the Exposition reflected the heritage of Spain and its colonial past as noted in a photo essay in Richard Pourade's *Gold in the Sun.* These buildings, along with Mission Revival structures such as the Santa Fe Depot, the Serra Museum, Naval Hospital, and the Marine Corps Recruit Depot left a permanent imprint on the city. From the arrival of Horton until this time, San Diego had architecturally been a Victorian town, with a few classical buildings thrown in. From this point on, the Hispanic origins of San Diego would be firmly established and either mission or Hispanic architecture would be a major feature of the city. It would help to give the unique flavor and identity to San Diego that would distinguish it from other cities in the nation of the same size. Photograph courtesy of the San Diego Historical Society—Ticor Collection

By the end of 1914, much had been done, both on the Exposition site and in the city as a whole. The Exposition was ready to open, and it did on January 1, 1915, when President Woodrow Wilson pressed a button which turned on a light hung from a balloon which illuminated an area of three square miles. Guns from the fort and naval vessels joined in, followed by fireworks from the organ pavilion in Balboa Park. For two years, a ticket to the Panama California Exposition admitted you to many delights. Photograph courtesy of the San Diego Historical Society Research Archives

Because of the late start and competition from San Francisco's international exhibition, San Diego's Exposition had limited international exhibits and only six states were represented. There were, however, exhibits from trade organizations, many western cities and counties, and exhibits stressing local concern. One example of the kind of exhibits the fair did attract was this Brazilian pavilion. Note that it is not a government exhibit, but is a "Private Exhibit..." The visitor in the center is former president Theodore Roosevelt, one of many distinguished visitors. Others were Henry Ford, Thomas A. Edison, and Assistant Secretary of the Navy Franklin Roosevelt and his wife Eleanor. The word those visitors carried back home, plus the fact that the Panama California Exposition was distinguished enough to attract such people to it, did much to publicize San Diego to the world. Photograph courtesy of the San Diego Historical Society—Ticor Collection

In addition to educational exhibits, the Panama California Exposition also provided entertainment. There were hula dancers and moving pictures and auto races between Barney Oldfield and Cliff Durant, and there was the midway, called the Isthmus, which featured a Chinatown, a large frog with toadstools on each side, and many other attractions of less than intellectual nature. One would like to think the absence of people would mean everyone was at the educational exhibits, but more likely the photograph was taken when the Exposition was not open to the public. Photograph courtesy of the San Diego Historical Society—Ticor Collection

This photograph illustrates two attractions of the Panama California Exposition—the Indian village and the menagerie. It also is significant for future reference, for that menagerie and that row of cages (center right, behind Indian Village) became the origins of the San Diego Zoo (see below). The Indian village was one of the more dramatic establishments at the Exposition. As explained in Lynn Adkins's article on the subject, the Santa Fe Railway built as a commercial exhibit the Painted Desert, which included a group of Zuni buildings, the Taos Pueblo, kivas, outdoor ovens, Navajo hogans, Apache teepees, all set in "rock" (actually wire frames covered with cement) to look like the Painted Desert. The photographs of the time show the reconstructions to have been amazingly accurate. After the Exposition the exhibit was used by the Boy Scouts, by the military in both world wars, was resurrected for the 1935 Exposition, and finally destroyed as unsafe in 1946. Photograph courtesy of the San Diego Historical Society—Ticor Collection

When the Panama California Exposition closed in 1916, what was left? First, a tremendous public relations success had brought the message of San Diego and its delights to millions around the world. The other thing left was a remarkable addition to Balboa Park. This 1915 photograph taken from a balloon shows the impact of the Exposition on the corner of the park (the rest was left as undeveloped open space). The Laurel Street bridge connected the Prado to the main part of the city. The Prado area with its stunning California Tower and a number of other baroque buildings were left standing. (This caused some problems over the years as none but the Tower had been designed to be permanent!) By stressing the Hispanic colonial style, the Balboa Park and the Exposition did much to turn San Diego back to its Hispanic roots and set the tone for the modern city. All in all, it must be recognized that the Exposition of 1915 was a major step toward San

Diego's designation as "America's Finest City." Photograph courtesy of the San Diego Historical Society—Ticor Collection

This dramatic photograph shows the destruction of the old Victorian Santa Fe Depot, with the new Mission Revival style building in the background. All of this was done in 1915, in preparation of the Panama California Exposition. Like the Goodhue-designed Spanish Colonial buildings of the Exposition, the Santa Fe station was an important step in moving the style of the San Diego building from Victorian frame and brick which looked like any other part of the country, to the Hispanic style which gives San Diego a unique identity. Photograph courtesy of the San Diego Historical Society—Ticor Collection

The second decade of the twentieth century was an extraordinary one for San Diego. Along with the Exposition and World War I, aviation came to town in a big way. San Diego became the "Air Capital" of the United States, with a long string of "firsts" in flying, flight schools, sea and amphibious planes, service facilities, and some of the biggest pioneer names in American aviation. The key figure was Glenn H. Curtiss who established a flying school on North Island in 1911. In three years he trained navy flyers,

civilians, obtained contracts for his airplanes, and developed a number of innovations in the new industry. One was the development of the first hydroplane (seaplane) which ever flew. Curtiss is shown here at the controls of that first seaplane, in 1912. With him on the plane is a Lieutenant Walker of the United States Army. Rockwell Field, established on North Island in 1914, became the "cradle of army aviation." Photograph courtesy of the San Diego Historical Society—Ticor Collection

It must always be remembered that the natural environment of San Diego is a desert. Like most deserts, that means there is usually not enough water, but when water comes, it comes in a flood. Never was that more true than in 1916. There had been a drought and the city more or less entered into a contract with well-known rainmaker Charles Hatfield to bring rain. The city was especially interested in enough rain to fill up the lake behind its new Morena Dam. Hatfield, shown mixing his mysterious rain-producing brew, went to work, and the rain did fall. Photograph courtesy of the San Diego Historical Society—Ticor Collection

For a time it looked like San Diego might become the capitol of lighter-than-air flight as well. The Troxel Company was organized and built a dirigible which had its maiden "flight" in November of 1912. Unfortunately, the sulfuric acid, water, and steel mixture did not produce enough hydrogen and the vessel would not fly. Wind damaged it and caused blockage of traffic at Thirty-first and "B" streets. When the inventor/manufacturer and his wife were murdered soon afterward by Troxel's secretary (it is not clear whether it was over money or over the secretary's wife's alleged affair with Troxel), the dirigible industry died in San Diego. Although the navy considered San Diego for naval dirigible bases well into the 1920s, it finally decided on another location. Photograph courtesy of the San Diego Historical Society—Ticor Collection

In 1916 the rains came—probably less as the result of the work of Charles Hatfield than because of very explainable climatic conditions. It began raining on January 5, with large rains again on January 10 and a real torrent on January 18. The Backcountry was severely flooded and the southern part of the county was especially affected. One dam, Lower Otay, was washed out completely, with heavy loss of life. The other southern dam, Sweetwater, was severely damaged. Mission Valley was flooded from side to side, with destruction of the concrete automobile bridge and, in the background, destruction of the railroad bridge, with a part of a train trapped on the remains. The town was thus isolated from land transportation to Los Angeles and the rest of the country, causing inconvenience for some time. Photograph courtesy of the San Diego Historical Society—Ticor Collection

Although the most extensive damage was in the Backcountry, the city itself did not escape floodwaters in 1916, as shown by the streetcar and automobiles moving through water at the intersection of Thirteenth and "M" streets on January 27, 1916. Most citizens of the city were outraged by the floods. Charles Hatfield, on the other hand, saw them as the mark of his success. After all, Morena Lake had been filled, as called for by his contract! He thus presented a bill for his services to the City Council. The Council denied there was a contract and refused to pay; a lawsuit continued until it was dropped by the courts in 1938. Individual suits against the city were also unsuccessful; the courts said that God and not Charles Hatfield had caused the rain! Photograph courtesy of the San Diego Historical Society—Ticor Collection

The American involvement in the First World War began shortly after the closing of the Panama California Exposition in 1916. The city immediately offered the vacant facilities and Balboa Park to the government for training facilities for the war effort. The Navy made heavy use of the park. In addition, they set up a tent hospital in the area of the present-day zoo, especially for recovering patients. These sailors on the Prado in 1916 are undoubtedly in a hurry to go stand in line somewhere. Photograph courtesy of the California State Library

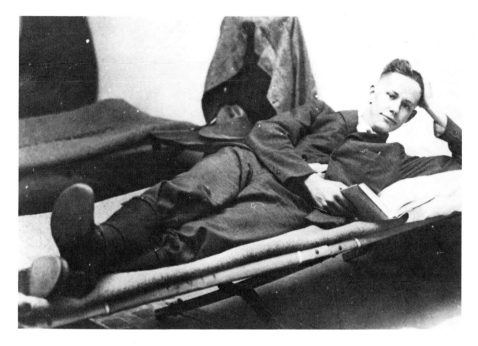

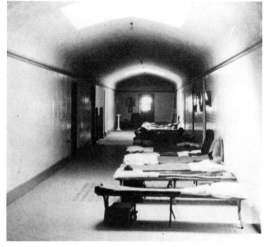

All kinds of San Diego public buildings were used to train soldiers in the First World War. One photograph shows the dormitory in the halls of San Diego High School; the other shows an unidentified soldier on his cot. He was one of the student-soldiers who trained at the building from October to December 1918. As explained by one of those soldiers, Jefferson K. Stickney, the students were members of a unit called the Student Army Training Corps (SATC) and consisted of ninety students, mostly from San Diego Junior College. They studied military law and military training at the high-school building. Photographs courtesy of the San Diego High School Alumni Association

The major training camp for the army was Camp Kearny, built for over $3 million on Linda Vista Mesa. The San Diego site was chosen because of the ideal weather conditions which would mean a minimum loss of working time because of bad conditions. The 9,466-acre camp included all facilities—housing, repair, hospitals, stores, and especially training. One of the most appropriate was this system of trenches designed to prepare the men for the most common feature of World War I fighting. Note also the bayonet-practice dummies suspended in the background. In the course of the war, over forty thousand people, mostly from the Southwestern states, were trained at Camp Kearny. Photograph courtesy of the Center for Regional History, San Diego State University

CAMP KEARNY MEN ON PERADE IN SAN DIEGO

This is a parade of soldiers from Camp Kearny marching in 1917 on Broadway, about Second Street. With all the training facilities in San Diego (in addition to Kearny, the Balboa Park facilities and the SATC, there was also the Naval Training Center and Rockwell Field), marching soldiers were a common sight. Mildred Adamson, who was a child at the time, remembers that she and other children would "wave at the soldiers marching by, covered with dust, carrying heavy equipment and guns. They were on their way to the harbor to go by ship to Europe . . . We probably are some of the last American children they saw as they glanced sideways at us and sadly smiled." Photograph courtesy of the San Diego Historical Society—Ticor Collection

Part of the patriotism of the war effort was focused on bond drives to finance the war. Celebrities of all sorts were called upon to push the sale of bonds. In 1918 famous cowboy movie star, William Hart, came to San Diego to sell bonds. Notice that this drive was to "Save Democracy," and to "Halt the Hun!" Photograph courtesy of the Center for Regional History, San Diego State University

World War I was accompanied by one of the world's worst influenza epidemics. It did not overlook San Diego. In 1918 and 1919 combined there were over 5,000 cases reported, with 368 deaths. This led to the closing of public schools, churches, theatres, and other public gatherings. People were expected to wear masks, as illustrated by these people in the Student Army Training Corps at San Diego High School. As one resident of the time recalls: "It hit San Diego very hard." Photograph courtesy of the San Diego Historical Society—Ticor Collection

Armistice was signed on November 11, 1918, halting one of the most bloody carnages in human history. To celebrate that event, the army assembled 212 aircraft from Rockwell and other nearby fields and conducted a massed flyover on November 27. It was both a fitting testimony to the end of the war, and a statement of the role of San Diego as the emerging "Air Capital" of the United States. Photograph courtesy of the Center for Regional History, San Diego State University

The 1910s were banner days for the Navy and the city; it can be said that San Diego's status as a "Navy Town" really dates from that decade. Naval aviation came to town in 1910; the first major warship, the 13,000-ton cruiser U.S.S. *California*, entered the harbor on December 4, 1910. Radio stations were established, as was an enlarged coaling wharf and a ship-yard. United States Marines arrived in 1914 under Joseph H. Pendleton and set up camp on North Island; in time that became the Marine Corps Re-cruit Depot. A submarine base, shown here, was set up in 1917 and in 1919 San Diego became the principal operating base of the Pacific Fleet. Photograph courtesy of the Los Angeles Public Library

The Marine Corps Recruit Depot, shown nearly completed in 1918, was built on "Dutch Flats" near the Bay. It came about when Congress-man William Kettner (a major factor in bringing the Navy build-up to San Diego) convinced Franklin Roosevelt, then assistant secretary of the Navy, of the virtues of the site when he came to San Diego to visit the Panama California Exposition. They selected 232 acres plus 500 acres of tidelands fill and hired the same architect who had designed the Exposition buildings to prepare the plans. It became still another example of Hispanic-influenced architecture which helped establish that form in San Diego. Photograph courtesy of the San Diego Historical Society—Ticor Collection

The Japanese became more and more important to San Diego. As indicated here, they were prominent in agriculture—especially truck farming and foodstuffs. The Japanese were equally important in the fishing industry, to which they made major contributions prior to their exclusion from fishing by racist government regulations and the Second World War. They introduced a flexible bamboo pole, barbless hooks, mass-produced lures, chumming, and refrigerated boats—all of which were important foundations for the tuna industry. Even their Portuguese competitors recognized their worth; one wrote: "The Japanese—they were the best of all fishermen." Photograph courtesy of the San Diego Historical Society—Ticor Collection

In 1919 San Diego's railroad east was finally finished. It ran over (and sometimes through) the mountains, across the desert to Yuma, and it fulfilled a dream that dated back to the 1850s. It brought a more direct connection with the national rail system, and it gave San Diego's port a chance to tap the produce of the Imperial Valley and the hinterland. The railroad was long-in-coming because of the difficult construction problems, such as this viaduct over Campo Gorge, and the even-more-forbidding Carrizo Gorge. Photograph courtesy of the UCLA Special Collections

The railroad was completed and on December 1, 1919, the first train left San Diego for the Imperial Valley. It was taken exclusively by the Klauber Wangenheim Company, as can be seen in the banners on the boxcars.

Although the train brought much promise to San Diego, it only brought limited benefits. It was frequently plagued by washouts caused by floods and by fires which damaged trestles and tunnels in times

of drought. After the 1970 floods it has been mostly closed down, probably permanently. Photograph courtesy of the Klauber Wangenheim Company

Many people think student demonstrations were invented in Berkeley in 1964. They were not; San Diego had one on June 6, 1918. The walkout was part of an extended controversy over the arbitrary actions of the School Board in refusing to renew the contracts of nineteen teachers at the high school. The board said "several of the teachers were under observation for pro-Germanism" and were fired for that reason. All public officials contacted denied that any teachers were under surveillance. When the board finally offered to reinstate some (eighteen) of the affected teachers, only three accepted. The others went elsewhere. It was a sorry "witch-hunting" blemish on San Diego's history, but not unusual in the United States during that period. Photograph courtesy of the San Diego Historical Society—Ticor Collection

The Panama California Exposition of 1915 did much to create local interest in the community, its identity, and its past. A 1912 organization, the Order of the Panama, founded to promote the exposition, was a major factor in that new concern for the community. In 1913 they searched and dug in the hillside around Presidio Hill for tiles from the old presidio, which they used to build a cross marking the site of Father Junipero Serra's original mission (see second photograph, showing the cross about 1918). At the same time a group of citizens led by George Marston bought the presidio site and covered the ruins with dirt in order to protect it all until the fort could be excavated, studied, and, they hoped, reconstructed. Photographs courtesy of the UCLA Special Collections and the San Diego Historical Society—Ticor Collection

President Woodrow Wilson visited on September 19, 1919. An overflow crowd of over fifty thousand gathered in the stadium in Balboa Park to hear Wilson speak in favor of the ratification of the Treaty of Versailles and the League of Nations. Pourade reports in *Gold in the Sun* that Wilson claimed rejection of the League of Nations would be a "death warrant to the children of the country!" This was the first overflow crowd in the new Balboa Stadium and the first time a new electric voice amplification system was used. Photograph courtesy of the San Diego High School Alumni Association

San Diego also became the center of the American film industry. With its clear air, good weather, and cheap locations, the area had everything the industry needed. A number of film companies were established in the county, the largest perhaps being the American Film Manufacturing Company (the Flying A) of Lakeside and La Mesa. Even after studios began to move to Hollywood, films were still made here. Because of the exotic buildings and landscaping, the Panama California Exposition buildings in Balboa Park were frequently used for the location of silent films. One was the film *The American,* made in 1916. The first photograph shows the camera crew at work filming on the Prado, with the California Tower in the background. The second picture shows what the cameramen saw, the battle in an imaginary Latin America banana republic. Photographs courtesy of the San Diego Historical Society—Ticor Collection

This striking night photograph of a biwinged plane flying over a Navy vessel on San Diego Bay is a good statement of much that had happened to the city in the 1910s. It had become the "Air Capital" of the United States and, as headquarters for the Pacific Fleet, one of the country's major "Navy Towns." The photograph is from a postcard, which was one of many ways in which the story of San Diego and its attractions was spread over the world in the decade of the 1910s. Photograph courtesy of the California State Library

This stylish "flapper" standing with foot on running board of an automobile
captures some of the spirit of San Diego in the twenties. There was Prohibition and "rum-running," and flappers, and gambling, and real estate
speculation, just as there was in much of the rest of the country. Photograph courtesy of the San Diego Historical Society—Ticor Collection

6

Forward Into The Twenties

—

In many respects the 1910s had been a magical decade for San Diego. In those ten years the city had made a commitment to the use of its Hispanic past as a means of creating a unique identity. It had launched an exposition which brought it international publicity, connections with major national figures, and created a turning point in its architectural history. San Diego had begun the harbor improvements needed to meet the challenges of increased Panama Canal traffic, and the city had finally gotten its direct railroad link to the east. San Diego had doubled in population and begun a pattern of almost unbroken growth which has continued to the present. The people developed many new cultural and social institutions, and strengthened old ones. Likewise, the city's Panama California Exposition did much to push forward the development of Balboa Park as one of the centerpieces of the city. The First World War had brought people and the military into the city on a large scale; with subsequent developments San Diego was well on the way to becoming a "Navy Town."

Throughout the decade of the 1920s, San Diego was on the march. The population doubled again, from 74,683 to 147,897, and the city grew in territory to accommodate the new people. Many major new subdivisions were started and old ones filled up; the city moved out of older sections of town (like Logan Heights and Golden Hills) into Kensington, Talmadge Park, University Heights, East San Diego, Mission Hills, Sunset Cliffs, and Pacific Beach. Many of the new subdivisions featured the new stucco and red tile construction with an Hispanic flavor. The emergence of the automobile as a major form of transportation also brought the beginning of strip development along such new thoroughfares as University Avenue.

The growth of the city was based upon continued expansion of San Diego's infrastructure. Although the need for water had been addressed in previous years with a number of reservoirs and distribution systems, the growth of the 1920s forced San Diego to build even more dams—Hodges, Barrett, Henshaw, Wohlford, Sutherland, and Lower Otay. Highway connections with the rest of the nation were established, especially after the difficult mountain grade through the eastern mountains was conquered, and a plank road was built over the desert sand dunes. The state and the county also began to improve many San Diego County roads, and even to pave the more important ones.

Port and harbor improvements began with the 1911 Capps Harbor Improvement Plan and were continued with the opening of the "B" Street Pier and additional facilities for the ever-increasing fishing industry. (The public had discovered it liked tuna, so the modern tuna-fishing industry began to emerge at this time). San Diego also

strengthened its commitment to the new world of aviation. Manned flight had come to San Diego in 1910, and the Curtiss School for flyers and the beginnings of military aviation had given it quite a boost in the 1910s. In the 1920s, San Diego citizen T. Claude Ryan created Ryan Airlines which offered the first regularly scheduled year-round air passenger service in the United States. He then moved into manufacturing and made it big when a young man named Charles A. Lindbergh asked him to build a plane for a solo flight across the Atlantic. After he became a major hero in his unfortunately named *Spirit of St. Louis,* San Diego named its new airfield after Lindbergh.

The decade of growth and prosperity brought a lot of changes in Balboa Park. In 1922, the city gave the Zoological Society land in the park. The society, which was formed right after the 1916 closing of the Panama California Exposition, began to build innovative exhibits and to collect animals from the world over. By the end of the decade the San Diego Zoo was a "world class" institution (even if they did not use the phrase in the 1920s). The San Diego Art Gallery also opened in Balboa Park, and plans were begun for the construction of the Natural History Museum, although it would not move into its new quarters until 1933.

Other developments in the city included the bringing of the sailing ship *Star of India* to town in 1927. In time it would become the core of the San Diego Maritime Museum, the second-most-important maritime museum in the West. Likewise, the Serra Museum was dedicated in its Mission-Revival glory in 1929, and its surroundings—now known as Presidio Park—were landscaped.

While all of these permanent additions to the scene were coming into being, the city was occupied with other things as well. In 1920 the Prince of Wales visited, and local citizens like to wonder if he met his future wife, Wallis

An indication of the lively nature of the 1920s in San Diego was the April 1920 visit of the next-in-line for the British throne, Edward, Prince of Wales. He was greeted by twenty-five thousand people at the stadium, and entertained lavishly at the banquet at the Hotel del Coronado. His future wife, Wallis Warfield Spencer, lived in San Diego at the time as a young navy wife. Years later when she was Wallis Warfield Spencer Simpson (having picked up still another husband along the way), she married Edward, and caused him to give up the British throne. Many San Diegans looked back on this 1920 event and wondered if they had met at the time. Photograph courtesy of the San Diego Historical Society—Ticor Collection

Less formal entertainment could also be found in Coronado. A tent city had been established in 1901, with dwellings, restaurants, a museum, bathing facilities, and entertainments of many varieties. The tent city remained popular until the growing use of automobiles began to draw people farther afield for their weekends and vacations. Coronado was still very popular in the 1920s, and these young women—flappers all—certainly seem to be enjoying themselves. Note cabana-type dwelling in the background. Photograph courtesy of the Center for Regional History, San Diego State University

Warfield Spencer (later Simpson was added), who was a very young navy wife in Coronado at the time. New beach areas were attracting both local residents and more and more out-of-town visitors. Prohibition made a large impact on the community—or, to be more precise, on San Diego's neighbor Tijuana. With both liquor and gambling available, Tijuana attracted thousands of Americans every day. Indeed, there are estimates that as many as one million Americans a year went from San Diego to Tijuana in the 1920s. In Tijuana they encountered horse racing, drinking, and many other pleasures. Although the movie-making industry had forsaken San Diego for Hollywood by the 1920s, many of the movie stars came back to town for the pleasure across the border.

While there was color and life and excitement in a growing San Diego, there were also some unpleasant aspects of the decade. For one thing the Ku Klux Klan was active here, as it was nationwide. It is difficult to know how large the local organization was or how extensive its activities were. Because of the small Afro-American, Jewish, and Roman Catholic population, it seems as though the nativism of the local Ku Klux Klan was less virulent than in some other parts of the country.

Thus San Diego, like the nation, was riding high in the 1920s, with speculation, growth, social experimentasion, and optimism. Unfortunately, serious problems lay underneath the surface and in San Diego, as in the rest of the nation, they came to the top in the 1930s.

It should not be assumed, however, that all women in San Diego in the twenties were decadent flappers. These women, riding in a 1921 parade, showed a more serious side of the period. There had long been a strong suffrage sentiment in San Diego, with Susan B. Anthony drawing a full house for a speech as far back as 1895. In the next year, San Diego County voted for a state constitutional amendment to grant women the vote, but the state as a whole defeated it. The Equal Suffrage Association worked hard to carry the 1911 state constitutional amendment and it did triumph statewide. San Diego leader Dr. Charlotte Baker was one of the first to register, and San Diego women voted for the first time in the 1911 city election. After the state-wide triumph, however, the Equal Suffrage Association stayed alive to work for the national suffrage, and as a political education group. That is why they were still parading in 1921, even though they had already won the vote. Photograph courtesy of the San Diego Historical Society-Ticor Collection

Sports and sports heroes were another feature of the twenties in the United States. San Diego showed its appreciation in 1925 when Jack Dempsey (barely visible behind the women) came to town to a most generous welcome. Photograph courtesy of the San Diego Historical Society-Ticor Collection

Prohibition in the United States did a lot to shape the 1920s in San Diego—or, to be more exact, in Tijuana. People went across the border for liquor and accompanying activities. In fact, at the peak of Prohibition one million people a year were going from San Diego to Tijuana. One of the major attractions was an elaborate new resort at Agua Caliente. It featured large club buildings housing gambling, a hotel, and drinking. There was also a quality racetrack. The number of automobiles in the parking lot would indicate it did very well, at least until 1935 when the Mexican government banned gambling and caused a considerable curtailment of American tourism to the border. Photograph courtesy of the San Diego Historical Society-Ticor Collection

With all interest in Prohibition, real estate development, growth of the Navy's presence and improvement of the port, one must not forget the continuation of cultural activities in San Diego during the 1920s. There were active musical groups, growing numbers of artists working in the city, and instruction in the dance. Much of that took place at the Ratliff Dance Studio in the second-story ballroom on Broadway and Eleventh Street. As can be seen, emphasis was on the new styles of the era. Isadora Duncan would have been pleased. Photographs courtesy of Jerry Hebert

The world famous San Diego Zoo got on its feet in the twenties. It had begun on October 2, 1916, when doctors Harry and Paul Wegeforth formed a society for a zoological garden. They began with animals which had been brought to the Panama California Exposition, and they also used cages left over from the fair. These temporary cages along Park Avenue housed the collection until 1922 when the zoo moved to its current site. If the bored look on the lion's face counts for anything, he was glad to move and get out of his little cage. Photograph courtesy of the San Diego Historical Society—Ticor Collection

The exertions of Dr. Harry Wegeforth and others finally pushed the city into providing Balboa Park land north of the Prado for a zoo. The area was considered worthless as it was barren and split by canyons. Many society members were horrified at the prospect, but not Dr. Wegeforth. He utilized that environment to advantage to build a zoo that displayed animals as naturally as possible. That meant open exhibits in the canyons, rather than box-like cages with bars on one side. The lion exhibit (paid for like so much else at the zoo by Ellen Browning Scripps) was one of the first and exemplifies the design the zoo would promote. As the 1926 *Zoonooz* put it, the lion grotto was "not a place to confine wild beasts, but a mounting designed to set off one of nature's masterpieces." Photograph courtesy of the San Diego Historical Society— Ticor Collection

By 1927 the zoo had developed to this point, as seen through a telephoto lens. In addition to exhibits like the lion grotto, there was the large bird cage seen on the left. This was the largest and the first of its kind in the world. The basic concept was to build a cage large enough to let the birds fly and live as naturally as possible—and then let the humans walk in the birds' midst. Almost everything seen in the photograph was built with money or supplies cadged by Dr. Wedgeforth—sometimes openly and sometimes not. (For instance, for years the zoo used city water acquired when Dr. Wegeforth simply tied into the water lines, without telling anyone at the city water offices.) Photograph courtesy of the San Diego Historical Society—Ticor Collection

Dr. Harry Wegeforth was clearly the "Founding Father" of the San Diego Zoo. Belle Benchley (right) was just as clearly the "Founding Mother." With no experience with zoos, she went to work as a bookkeeper in 1922, and showed such remarkable administrative and public relations skills that Dr. Wegeforth insisted she be appointed director in 1926. She was the first woman director of a major zoo anywhere. Benchley presided over the zoo until her retirement at age seventy in 1952. She is shown with Osa Johnson who, with her husband Martin, brought many specimens to the zoo, along with Frank "Bring Them Back Alive" Buck, and Dr. Wegeforth himself, who organized many collecting expeditions for the zoo. Photograph courtesy of the San Diego Historical Society—Ticor Collection

150

Mission Beach had long been a very popular beach for San Diegans. It acquired an additional attraction in the 1920s with the opening of an entertainment complex developed by John D. Spreckels in order to attract riders to his streetcar system. The centerpiece was the roller coaster, seventy-five feet high, with a long line waiting to try it on opening day, July 4, 1925. Other attractions included a large swimming pool, a boardwalk, and a dance hall. Slightly to the north, a series of cabins were built out on Crystal Pier, which also proved popular. Some San Diego people summered at the site, and others simply came for the day on Spreckels's streetcar or by private auto. Photograph courtesy of the San Diego Historical Society Public Library Collection

As Charles Wright and Faye Baird Fraser show us on December 28, 1926, the roller coaster was not the only thing to attract people to Mission Beach. The activity called "sport surfing" had recently arrived from Hawaii, although it would not be the mass sport we now know until the 1960s and the advent of cheaper, lighter and more-maneuverable boards. Photograph courtesy of the San Diego Historical Society—Ticor Collection

The 1920s were marked throughout the country by a massive surge of fundamentalist religion. This surge brought a number of new churches and movements, as well as increased activity among traditional fundamentalist sects, as exemplified by the Scopes Monkey Trial in Tennessee. California was noted for new cults which appeared and did much to create the image of California as a place different from the rest of the United States. One such cult was led by Aimee Semple McPherson, who preached the Four Square Gospel. She built a huge temple in Los Angeles, stressed a theology of love and hope, and drew huge crowds with gossamer gowns, bands, and colorful lighting. She also came to San Diego. She is shown here around 1920 in Balboa Park praying over a sick child. Later in her career she was involved in a mysterious "kidnapping," during which she claims to have been held captive in San Diego. Photograph courtesy of the San Diego Historical Society—Ticor Collection

The upsurge in religious interest in the 1920s was not confined to fundamentalists or new and unique cults. There was a general growth in religious activity which historians and sociologists explain by noting the tensions created in the country by all the changes taking place: the changed social situation of women, with short hair and shorter skirts, smoking, working outside the home; the more-mobile population with the automobile; changed racial living patterns; disruptions of families as people moved from the rural family-oriented world of an older America to an urban world with much less sense of community. In response to those tensions, many turned to religion to seek an anchor. It is possible that is one of the reasons why the site for hillside sunrise services at Mt. Helix was completed at this time, 1925. Photograph courtesy of the San Diego Historical Society—Ticor Collection

This 1933 photograph of an initiation ceremony, probably of San Diego Klan No. 64, shows that the Ku Klux Klan existed in San Diego in this period. This followed the national pattern, although it does not appear that the local Klan was as virulent as those of other parts of the nation. Because of the secrecy inherent in the organization, it is hard to pin down its exact size and role. One small collection of Klan papers gives some hints. A partial notebook lists fifty-one names and addresses of what may be a membership list; furthermore there is frequent correspondence from the national organization regarding the need to regenerate the local chapter. It is also hard to know what their activities were. Actor Gregory Peck has said that one of his earliest memories of childhood in La Jolla was the burning of a cross on the lawn of a home rented by an Afro-American family. An undated questionnaire asking members what programs they would like the local Klan to pursue says little about racism, but stressed watching the local governmental officials to see that there is clean government and lower taxes. Some do mention "exterminate the agitator" and "deport all aliens." Photograph courtesy of the San Diego Historical Society—Ticor Collection

Not only did the Ku Klux Klan have a chapter in San Diego; it even had a women's auxiliary! A local women's membership card for 1929 is shown here, along with the *Constitution and Laws* and an open page of the *Kloran or Ritual of the Women of the Ku Klux Klan*, 1928 version. Note the questions asked to prospective members. They are designed to be sure the member is white, Christian, and owes no loyalty to anyone other than the United States. Such regulations would effectively exclude non-whites, Jews, and Roman Catholics. At this time, there is no way to ascertain the effectiveness or extent of the Women's Ku Klux Klan in San Diego in the 1920s. Photograph courtesy of the San Diego Historical Society Research Archives

Another national trend of the twenties which manifested itself in San Diego was the preservation of historic shrines. The *Star of India* was brought to town in 1927, the lighthouse on Point Loma was soon to be restored, and work was started on restoration of the church building at Mission San Diego de Alcala. Preliminary efforts and some fund raising had been done earlier, culminating in some preservation of the church facade in 1919 under the leadership of George Marston. Fuller restoration of the 1813 mission church began in 1927 when Alfred Mayrhofer, with full support of the Roman Catholic bishop for the area, John J. Cantwell, organized a major effort. Money was raised from the community and the

Church, but lost when the bank in which it was deposited failed. More money was then raised and ground was broken in 1930 on a project which involved rebuilding the badly-decomposed church. The project was completed and dedicated with two days of ceremony in September 1931. Photograph courtesy of the San Diego Historical Society—Ticor Collection

If anything captured the essence of the twenties, it was the automobile. The automobile was helpful in running illegal liquor. It brought social mobility to the country and disrupted many extended families. It encouraged development of suburbs. The automobile gave women a new freedom and began to change their life in many ways. San Diego was, even more than the country as a whole, becoming tied to the automobile. The view of Sixth and "C" streets in 1924 shows the way it was becoming a part of downtown. Can you find a vacant parking place in this photograph? Photograph courtesy of the San Diego Historical Society—Ticor Collection

On July 16, 1929, the 160th anniversary of Father Serra's establishment of the mission on Presidio Hill, the people of San Diego dedicated the Serra Museum on that same hill. It was to house the San Diego Historical Society, which had been incorporated in 1928 with George Marston the first president and the leading force. He, with others, had acquired the historic site of Presidio Hill over the years and had hired William Templeton Johnson to design the museum. Johnson designed one of the finest examples of Mission

Revival architecture in town; unfortunately it is so good that many tourists and not a few locals think the museum *is* the old mission. This 1929 photograph is taken from Old Town on dedication day and shows the new Serra Museum, the Serra Cross and Serra Palm on the horizon, and the large opening-day crowds. It also gives a good idea of the relationship of the Old Town to the original presidio site. Photograph courtesy of the San Diego Historical Society—Ticor Collection

As San Diego grew in the 1920s, the automobile was the main vehicle, and highways were necessary for it. Major routes had been secured in the previous decade, and now it was time to pave them. The most important highway event of this decade was the completion of the paving of U.S. Highway 101 from San Diego to Los Angeles. Among other things, that brought San Diego within reach of the population of the Los Angeles basin and greatly increased tourism in San Diego. These "before" and "after" photographs of Highway 101 give an idea of the advantages of the paving of that highway. The first shows the unpaved Highway 101, close to the beach at Cardiff in 1914; the second shows the newly paved road at Carlsbad (not too far from the site of the first photograph) in 1927. Photographs courtesy of the San Diego Historical Society—Ticor Collection

San Diego continued to grow in the 1920s, both in population and in size. This growth tended to feature several things: automobile oriented "strip development"; heavy use of Spanish or Mission Revival architecture; and land speculation such as was going on at a national level. This 1928 photograph of University Avenue about Thirtieth Street illustrates the first point. With the growing use of the car, neighborhoods lost their cohesion; no longer was it necessary to group services and stores in neighborhoods close to a streetcar stop or within walking distance. Instead development—especially commercial—was built along strips of major streets. These "strips" might go on for miles, as they did on University Avenue and El Cajon Boulevard, the best examples of strip development in San Diego. It was the beginning of a world in which one would be almost totally incapacitated without an automobile. Photograph courtesy of the San Diego Historical Society—Ticor Collection

Tourism in the 1920s, stimulated by continual publicity campaigns, continued to grow in San Diego. Automobile tourism was still, however, rather primitive. The first photograph shows the municipal campgrounds in Balboa Park in 1923, and is pretty typical of the way many tourists travelled at that time. Note the rolled up mattress on the front fender. As the decade progressed, accommodations began to pick up with the new institution, the tourist court, or auto camp. The tourist camp was really just an elaboration on the campsite. They were built along the highways, usually on the outskirts of town, and featured simple rooms, sometimes with individual plumbing and sometimes without. This one, Young's Modern Auto Court, was located at 2822 San Diego Avenue "on 101, Historic Old Town, by Ramona's Marriage Place." First photograph courtesy Los Angeles Public Library, and the second courtesy of the UCLA Special Collections

Subdivisions of residences continued to be opened, as they had since Horton's day. After the Exposition of 1915, however, they were usually built in either Spanish or Mission Revival styles (or a mixture of both). Stimulated by the Panama California Exposition, the Santa Fe Depot, the Serra Museum, MCRD, the Naval Hospital and others, a Hispanic style with white stucco, arches, and red tile roofs became a statement of San Diego. Indeed, contemporary references in the 1920s and 1930s often referred to San Diego as "that little Spanish town by the bay with its Spanish style stucco and red tile roofs." An example of such development which occurred in the 1920s would be Kensington Heights. Notice that every house in this 1928 picture is stucco and has some element of Hispanic architecture. Notice also the tiny palm and eucalyptus trees. The developer had planted acacia, but the residents tore them out and planted the area with Mediterranean-style trees. Photograph courtesy of the San Diego Historical Society—Ticor Collection

This somewhat fuzzy relief map shows the extent of the city's development by the mid-1920s. Essentially the area between present day Interstate 8 and State Highway 94 on the north and south; and Interstate 5 and Fairmount Avenue on the west and east, has been filled in. In addition, outer areas such as Sunset Cliffs, Pacific Beach, La Jolla, and National City are also well defined. Most of the city up to this point was laid out in the traditional American-style city squares—regardless of the terrain. With the development of new concepts of suburban design in the 1920s, that would change. Most of the city laid out after this period has been developed with curving streets, cul-de-sacs, and some reference to the natural terrain. This picture/map thus shows San Diego at the end of one era of city design and on the brink of the next. Photograph from John Nolen, *City Plan for San Diego, California* (1926)

While much of the San Diego economy was built on tourism, commerce at the port, and the military, it must be remembered that San Diego was also a regional service and trade center. One example of that would be the vinegar works of the Klauber Wangenheim Company, a regional wholesale food distributor. The company packaged a wide variety of food stuffs in their own labels (*Point Loma* for canned goods and *Silver Gate* for vinegar) for sale to their regional customers. Here are E. T. Brown, Bill Copeland, and Marin Smith in the vinegar area in Klauber Wangenheim's manufacturing department at Fourth and Market Streets, 1928. Photograph courtesy of the Klauber Wangenheim Company

The United States Navy continued to be a major presence in the city; indeed it increased its role in this decade. For one thing it established a large destroyer repair base, shown here in 1923. Many of these vessels eventually ended up in the mothball fleets, to be traded to England in the Destroyer Deal in 1940. The Navy also continued many training activities in the area. As late as 1928 they were still using facilities in Balboa Park. One facility used was the lily pond, which the Navy utilized for boating and survival training. Photographs courtesy of the San Diego Historical Society—Ticor Collection

159

The Navy hospital began in 1917 as a dispensary in one of the old exposition buildings in Balboa Park. It evolved into the Navy Hospital, housed in this building shown as of 1925. The building was also designed in a modified Hispanic architectural style and thus blended well with the remaining exposition buildings a few blocks away. San Diego has long had pride in its Navy Hospital, at least until the 1970s when the Navy insisted in taking additional Balboa Park land for a new hospital—despite the wishes of many San Diegans that no more park land should be used. Photograph courtesy of the San Diego Historical Society—Ticor Collection

More aviation "firsts" occurred in America's "Air Capital" in the 1920s. One was the first refueling in flight, which took place in 1923 over the Spanish Bight between North Island and Coronado. In the top plane were Lt. Frank Seifer and Lt. Virgil Kine. In the lower aircraft were Lt. John P. Richter and Capt. Lowell H. Smith. Frank Seifer became a city councilman and was the first to land at the new (1928) Lindbergh Field. Photograph courtesy of the San Diego Historical Society—Ticor Collection

San Diego's title of "Air Capital of America" has originally been based upon military aviation and a long string of "firsts," ranging from the first seaplane to the first barrel roll. In the 1920s, San Diego moved further into the aviation future with the creation in 1925 of Ryan Airlines organized by T. Claude Ryan and B. Franklin Mahoney. They built up a fleet of fifteen airplanes and inaugurated regular service between San Diego and Los Angeles. Ryan was not satisfied with the equipment available and he sold out to Mahoney and devoted himself primarily to design and manufacture. The plane which gave his company a real start was a monowing called the "M-1" and the first was tested on February 1, 1926. When the precursor of United Air Lines bought seven of them, the future of Ryan's aircraft manufacturing company was set. An example of that M-1 Ryan aircraft is shown here. Photograph courtesy of the San Diego Historical Society—Ticor Collection

Where, except in the "Air Capital of the United States," would Santa Claus arrive in an airplane, to be greeted in December by bathing beauties (or at least what passed for "beauties" at the time!) at Mission Beach, circa 1925. Photograph courtesy of the San Diego Historical Society—Ticor Collection

The biggest thing that happened to San Diego aviation was Charles A. Lindbergh, who selected a Ryan aircraft designed and manufactured in San Diego for his transatlantic flight. He came to San Diego in 1927 to supervise the construction and modification of the plane, and then to test it. Much of the plane was constructed in an abandoned cannery near the Ryan factory and airport. This is the fuselage being assembled outside the factory. Photograph courtesy of the San Diego Historical Society—Ticor Collection

The completed plane is shown with the people who built her assembled in front. Charles A. Lindbergh is seventh from the left, towering a head higher than most of the others. There are still many people in San Diego who remember working on that airplane. When it was necessary to build a new model of the craft to replace one destroyed by fire in the Aerospace Museum, a number of the original workers were still in San Diego and worked on the replica, which was made from the original plans. Photograph courtesy of the San Diego Historical Society—Ticor Collection

This is Charles A. Lindbergh in the *Spirit of St. Louis* leaving for his trip to Paris. San Diegans like to think of this takeoff as simply the first leg of that historic 1927 flight. After the famous flight, Lindbergh returned to the city and was greeted with adoration. There were parades, speeches, banquets, and the city bathed in the reflected glory of the twenties' greatest hero. Photograph courtesy of the San Diego Historical Society—Ticor Collection

So enamored was San Diego with Charles A. Lindbergh that when the new airport was completed in 1928, it was named Lindbergh Field. It was built upon landfill to meet the needs of both air traffic and the growing cluster of aircraft manufacturing establishments coming to town. This flyover was part of the opening day ceremonies, which appears to have been well attended. Photograph courtesy of the San Diego Historical Society—Ticor Collection

One of the signs in the window makes a good title for this Depression
photograph: "On the rocks of Depression." Although the extensive
government payrolls in the area meant San Diego suffered less than some
parts of the nation, it still suffered during the Depression. Again and again
survivors say almost the same thing: "Oh, it was terrible," "it was really
hard times for lots of people," "it was pretty bad," and "there was a great
deal of need." The loss of jobs, of homes, and of businesses were among
the more depressing effects of the Depression of many San Diegans. Photograph courtesy of the San Diego Historical Society—Ticor Collection

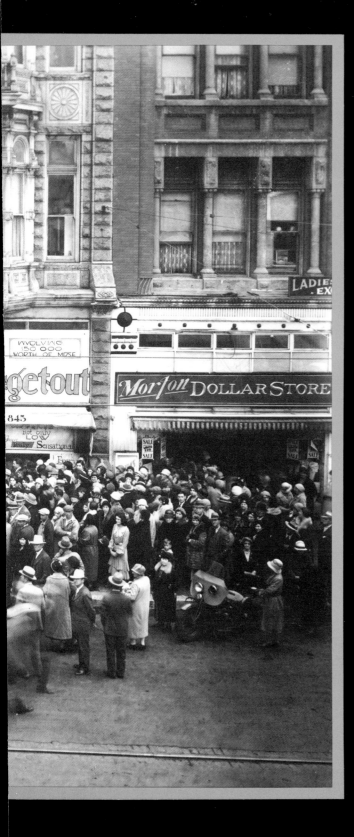

7
The Depression In San Diego 1929-1941

T he Wall Street Crash occurred in October of 1929 and the Great Depression followed immediately. The effect on San Diego was a little delayed. As Marston Burnham noted, "We were always a little behind everything in San Diego than they were in the East and it generally took us a year or two to catch up or down." The Depression did, however, "catch up" and the economy did turn "down"—severely. At the same time, there were factors which softened the Depression in San Diego as there were other factors which brought not only a faster recovery, but a boom by the end of the decade.

That is not to say, however, that the Depression was not severe in San Diego. It hurt in a lot of ways. By 1930 building permits were down by 50 percent and it took newspapers sixty-five pages just to list all the delinquent taxpayers. Unemployment was 16,000 by 1932 and 23,000 by 1933 (out of a population of about 150,000). Even though the percentage of unemployed people was somewhat less than the national average, the Depression still hurt and hurt some badly.

In addition to unemployment and business failures, many people—especially in the middle-class—lost their homes and businesses. Others lost all their savings and investments in stocks and bonds. There were many destitute people who were cared for primarily by charities. The charities provided basic necessities and gave some people money to return to the Midwest whence they had come. At one point, Catholic charities used a system of meal tickets which were honored by some restaurants. There also was a ticket system for people who had to sleep at the Salvation Army. One resident at the time still remembers the suffering: "Some of them you are sorry about. It just makes me sick to look at them. Their eyes tell you—you tell by a person's eyes if they're hungry and they're sick and they're tired."

The migrants coming to the area—called "Oakies" although they were often from Texas, Oklahoma, Nebraska, Kansas, and even the Dakotas—added to the problem. Although it is impossible to know how many came to San Diego the number seems to have been large. Richard Pourade reports in *The Rising Tide* that in 1935 a combined government-private assistance program was set up and 696 applied in one month. Their problems were compounded by the hostility of the locals to people who were from poor and backward areas. As one resident noted, "the Oakies did not even know what a flush toilet was; they thought it was to wash your feet in!"

The Depression in San Diego seems to have reached bottom in 1934. By that time a number of federal programs were set up which helped alleviate the misery and perhaps they helped bring some of the recovery. The programs included the Civilian Conservation Corps (CCC), and especially the Works Progress Administration (WPA). Many projects were launched in the community. A baseball field was built, a new State College, and several million dollars were spent for harbor and waterfront improvements. There was an opera project, a city schools curriculum project, some work at the agricultural district's fairgrounds, and several projects in conjunction with the 1935 California Pacific International Exposition. The Civil Works Administration (CWA) provided jobs for thousands. The national government also spent additional millions in the area on military construction and for a new $755,000 post office building. Other construction—not always New Deal projects—also contributed to the recovery. That would include improvements on the water system, a new highway through Rose Canyon and the lengthening and improving of Broadway Pier. Lindbergh Field and Balboa Park were improved and El Capitan Dam begun.

The first Exposition in Balboa Park had been developed at least partly to get the city moving again after the recession of the early 1900s—and it seems to have worked. Why not do it again? The city did, staging a large fair in 1935 and 1936, which utilized much of what was left from the 1915 Exposition in Balboa Park, and added new buildings and new attractions. Although it lacked some of the charm and long range impact of the Panama California Exposition, it was still a success, both in drawing visitors (over seven million), and in publicizing San Diego and its attractions.

By 1935 San Diego was definitely on an upswing. There was the continually growing tuna industry, tourism, and the return of local construction and growth. But most important, the late 1930s in San Diego were shaped by the aircraft industry, and by the pre-World War II buildup. As Marston Burnham remembered it, the key to recovery was "when Consolidated first came here

166

As 1930 came upon San Diego, the city was beginning to look like a city. This photograph of the San Diego High School entry marching down Broadway in the Armistice Day Parade clearly shows that. To the left is the Pickwick Hotel; somewhat behind that with the twin radio transmitters is the U.S. Grant Hotel (then still the city's finest) with the San Diego Trust and Savings Bank in the background. On the right side of the street is the Bank of America skyscraper. The rapid growth of the two previous decades was slowed considerably by the Depression, but by the end of the 1930s it was resumed with the maturing of the aircraft industry and the increase in the military presence because of the oncoming world war. Photograph courtesy of the San Diego High School Alumni Association

One of the national tragedies of the Depression was the collapse of thousands of banks, taking down with them the working capital and savings of millions of people. Generally speaking, San Diego banks were sound and, although there were failures, the distress here was less than elsewhere. San Diego banks did, however, have to close for the national Bank Holiday, and they did have to work under severe restrictions for a brief time. The bank runs and other problems of other areas never became problems here; quite the contrary, when the banks opened after the Bank Holiday, there was actually a surplus of cash on hand. Ironically, the bank shown with the Depression-era crowd in front survived the Depression to collapse in 1973. Photograph courtesy of the San Diego Historical Society—Ticor Collection

[1935]. That, I think started an upswing and from then until the war things were very active in San Diego. Business was good." Consolidated Air joined Solar and Ryan for the aircraft boom. Consolidated alone brought increased building permits and more than three-thousand new jobs by 1936. After 1935 Ryan's orders tripled and Solar Aircraft sold large quantities of aircraft components. Coupled with the military expansion taking place in San Diego, the city had gone from Depression to Boom by 1939.

San Diego also grew in numbers in the 1930s. The population in the 1930 census had been a little under 150,000. By the census of 1940 it was up to 203,341 and by the summer of 1941, it was likely closer to 250,000. The phenomenal role of the aircraft industry in producing that is emphasized by Richard Pourade when he notes that in 1928 there were 232 people working in the aviation industry, and by 1941 there were 20,000. Even before Pearl Harbor, San Diego had become a war camp and one of the major builders of the United States' war machine.

Locally, as nationally, real estate speculation had been a major part of the prosperity of the 1920s. The collapse of real estate booms was a major part of the Crash of 1929 and the Depression. In San Diego a good example was Point Loma. John P. Mills had come to town with four hundred dollars and quickly made six million dollars. He developed the Sunset Cliffs region, laying out streets and in 1926 building the Mills Mansion (forecenter), one of the showplace residences of San Diego. With the Crash, he lost everything, including the mansion which was sold at auction. As he put it: "I had nothing but money once. Then I had nothing." His sentiments, coupled with this 1930 photograph of all the unsold lots in his defunct development, tell much of the effects of the Depression on San Diego. Photograph courtesy of the California Historical Society Library, San Francisco

Native Americans in San Diego County have suffered deprivation, poverty, and cultural stress ever since the white man arrived on the scene. Although some, like the Kumeyaay in the eastern Backcountry, avoided the mission experience, they did suffer extreme poverty and cultural disruption in the late nineteenth and early twentieth centuries. Yet, as local historian Stephen Van Wormer has noted, "In spite of the drastic acculturation experienced by the Eastern Kumeyaay . . . the group has persisted as a cultural entity." An example of that cultural persistence is shown in this snapshot taken in 1935 at Anahuac by a photographer known only as "Kelly." The picture shows Kumeyaay men playing the traditional Indian guessing and gambling game called "peon." Photograph courtesy of the San Diego Museum of Man

The Depression was at its worst in San Diego from 1931 to 1934, after that things began to turn up. Some relief and perhaps some impetus to that upturn came from various federal programs, such as the Works Progress Administration, which built a number of public facilities, and the Civilian Conservation Corps, shown here working on the restoration of the lighthouse for the Cabrillo National Monument. The Monument had been created in 1913 and was centered around the decayed 1854 lighthouse. The CCC refurbished the lighthouse, added a garage, comfort station, retaining wall and bronze plaque commemorating Cabrillo's voyage. It was all dedicated on September 28, 1935. Photograph courtesy of the Cabrillo National Monument

A number of San Diego citizens still recall the effects of the Crash of 1929 and the Depression which followed. These remembrances are from oral history interviews at the San Diego Historical Society:

Oh, it was terrible. Everybody we knew was affected in some way. . . . People didn't have so many of the things they have now; they didn't have unemployment insurance and they didn't have Social Security. . . Medicare. . .Medi-Cal. You went on the County and you were treated atrociously. You were made ashamed that you didn't have a job. . . .

Jeanne Rimmer

My brother, who was a Rhodes Scholar. . .took a job at the Ford building [in the 1935 Exposition] helping to demonstrate how the Ford car went through the assembly line. He did this because there were no jobs available for anybody who was as qualified as he was. So it really was hard times for lots of people. . .My father lost our home along with everything else. . . .

Katherine Taylor

I was twenty. Jobs were scarce and a lot of the boys went into the CCC— Civilian Conservation Corps—and girls would, if they could, get a job in the dime store at twelve dollars a week. There was no minimum wage then, I think. It was hard on girls. . . because of so many of the employers took advantage of the fact that those girls *had* to have those jobs, and there was sexual harassment, a lot of it. My father didn't want me to work in an office; he knew too much about what happened. I am sure it was much more common than it could be nowadays.

Jeanne Rimmer

Well, that's when the stock market crashed you know and it was awful. It was tough on us, we lost everything, too. . . . Well, my husband was only out of work about two weeks as I told you. We lost all our investments in the bank and our stocks and things just went up in smoke like everybody else's.

Marie Mayrhofer

Well, it was pretty bad. During that period of the Depression, of course, it'd come on gradually and I remember I anticipated and I had one thousand dollars in cash so when they closed all the banks, I helped many of my friends out who didn't have any cash. It was really tough. There was very little law business—there was law business, but nobody could pay for it. So I went up to the San Joaquin Valley where they dug oil wells and got money that way.

Charles Forward

Then, of course, in '33, we got into the depths of the Depression when Roosevelt was President. I went down there [to the bank] one day in March. . .well, there was a telegram there from the Comptroller of Currency (Federal) which said, "Under Executive Order all banks [were] to remain closed until further notice." I looked at that thing and I got ahold of Mr. Belcher. . .I said, "We've got plenty of money, we're not going to close, are we?" "Andy," he said, "if you don't obey that order either the president or the cashier will be going to jail and I'm not going to jail. Don't you open the bank!". . .They let us pay ten dollars every three days, I think it was, to the families so they could get bread and butter and then we cleared the drafts on the perishables. . . .

Anderson Borthwick

San Diego State College was another institution which benefited from New Deal relief programs. They financed the new campus for the college. It was designed in the Mission Revival style architecture so popular in the period, and opened in 1931 on Montezuma Mesa in the eastern part of the city. The completed but still raw campus is shown in 1934. Even then, cost was a matter of concern. Katherine Taylor reports that when she attended from 1929 to 1933, it cost ten dollars a month to meet all expenses. Photograph courtesy of the San Diego State University Archives

While the Depression held the nation in its grip, the people coped as best they could. One thing which helped divert their attention from their misery was the 1932 Olympics, held in Los Angeles. San Diego had a special reason to cheer, as one of their own, San Diego High School and Stanford University track star, Bill Miller (shown here in a 1929 high school picture) won the gold medal in the pole vault. He set an Olympic record as well, vaulting 14′, 1¾″. Sports have always been important to San Diegans and the city has turned out many major figures such as Maureen "Mo" Connolly, Ted Williams, Archie Moore, Florence Chadwick, Marcus Allen, Greg Louganis, Billy Casper, and Bill Walton. Photograph courtesy of the San Diego High School Alumni Association

While most of the country backed Franklin Roosevelt's administration and its efforts to improve life, not all did. He was severely attacked by both the extreme right and the extreme left. An example of a leftist attack was the Communist Party Rally held on May 30, 1933. When Los Angeles officials denied the Young Communist League a parade permit, they converged instead on San Diego. They proceeded to attack Roosevelt and the military establishment for their part in contributing to the evils of the world. The league was met by the San Diego police and a conflict followed with injuries to both police and demonstrators. Eight demonstrators were jailed and the rest were escorted to the city limits. Photograph courtesy of the San Diego Historical Society—Ticor Collection

171

This assemblage of elderly people photographed on June 2, 1934, was involved in the Townsend movement in San Diego. The movement was based on a plan to provide a two hundred dollar federal pension to the elderly, with the requirement that the money be spent within thirty days. That would both help the older citizens and pump money into the stagnant economy. As Paul Lucas, historian of the local Townsend activities, noted, the movement was strong in San Diego, especially from 1934 through 1936 when local Republicans used the movement to help retain political power. By early 1935, there were seventy-two Townsend Clubs in the county, and within three months, they obtained sixty-thousand signatures on petitions. The clubs were instrumental in the election of a local congressman, a state senator, several assemblymen, and the mayor. Photograph courtesy of the San Diego Historical Society— Ticor Collection

In 1935 San Diego tried to pull itself out of the Depression with another exposition. This one would be called the California Pacific International Exposition, and would use much of the 1915-1916 site of the Panama California Exposition in Balboa Park, with some additional buildings, exhibits, and gardens. New structures would include a Spanish Village, a group of small houses which came to be known as the House of Pacific Relations, and a replica of Shakespeare's Old Globe Theatre. Hollywood lighting experts were called in to design new lighting for the fair. It is obvious from this 1935 construction scene, that the fair not only helped San Diego come out of the Depression by serving to publicize the city; it also helped in the long run by providing much needed construction jobs. Photograph courtesy of the Security Pacific National Bank Collection/Los Angeles Public Library

This publicity photograph of Florence Kelton in romanticized Spanish costume standing in the still-under-construction Federal Building with the San Diego skyline in the background, explains what the 1935 California Pacific International Exposition was about: publicity. Oscar W. Cotton, one of the major backers of the exposition, argued that "With this exposition fifty thousand dollars in advertising will do more for San Diego, to put us again in the limelight of the world, than would one million dollars without the Exposition. Never has San Diego had such an opportunity." Considering that home building starts reached a low of six in August 1934, San Diego could use the publicity. Photograph courtesy of the Security Pacific National Bank Collection/Los Angeles Public Library

The purposes of the California Pacific International Exposition were varied—publicity, entertainment, and education. These sculptures and the "Mural of Education," were photographed June 12, 1935. They illustrate some of the educational material at the fair. Both the sculptures and the mural also illustrate the Depression-era styles of a sort which were duplicated around the country in hundreds of courthouses, post offices, and other public buildings. Photograph courtesy of the Security Pacific National Bank Collection/Los Angeles Public Library

The 1935 California Pacific International Exposition had its merits, but it lacked the charm and class of the 1915 Exposition. For one thing, it included a nudist colony. That is what is behind this fence, and that is what the three men are photographing. One wonders—was the railing built there for that purpose? The expression on the passing matron's face would suggest that not everyone at the Exposition approved of this part of the fair. Photograph courtesy of the San Diego Historical Society—Ticor Collection

If one were to stand on the rail shown in the previous photo (or paid the admission cost and went inside)—this is what they would have seen. The attack on Victorianism which had been part of the twenties seems to have been at least somewhat victorious! Is this why over 7,200,000 visited the California Pacific International Exposition in 1935 and 1936? Photograph courtesy of the San Diego Historical Society—Ticor Collection

If the nudist exhibit was a little too much for the exposition visitor, they could always visit the Midget Village. There they could see midgets living and posing in a variety of situations, including having tea with a group of elephants. There was also a tightrope-walking goat. Photograph courtesy of the San Diego Historical Society—Ticor Collection

It must not be assumed that there were *no* serious exhibits at the California Pacific International Exposition. There were many, including this entire mall which included Electricity and Varied Industries on the left, the California State Building on the right, and the Ford Building at the end. In the Ford Building, one could see an exhibit showing the process whereby Ford automobiles were manufactured on the Ford Motor Company's assembly line. The building, by Exposition Architect Richard Regua, was meant to exemplify the best in modern industrial design. Photograph courtesy of the San Diego Historical Society—Ticor Collection

A major purpose of the Exposition was national publicity. What would be more effective in obtaining national publicity than a visit from the president of the United States? Franklin and Eleanor Roosevelt came to visit on October 2, 1935. In his speech, President Roosevelt hailed the California Pacific International Exposition as an indication that things were turning around and the economy improving. Photograph courtesy of the San Diego High School Alumni Association

Although the Depression did bring considerable suffering to San Diego, it did not bring the community to a complete halt. Furthermore, military and other spending helped San Diego come out of the Depression sooner than much of the rest of the country. This 1936 or 1937 view of the "B" Street Pier area illustrates that. Tied up along the Embarcadero is the *Lake Frances* of Tacoma with a load of lumber—which indicates that building was being resumed. To its right is an Omaha-class light cruiser, with a liner, probably a United States Line vessel, behind it. Photograph courtesy of the Maritime Museum of San Diego

In addition to commerce and fishing, shipbuilding and repair were important to the San Diego harbor. One major establishment was the Campbell Machine Company, which began soon after 1900 as a general machine shop repairing cars, steam and gas engines. It eventually dropped automobiles and concentrated on shipbuilding. Photographer Passmore cleverly managed to include his automobile in this photograph which shows the "Mariner Hull #29" being framed. Photograph courtesy of the San Diego Historical Society—Ticor Collection

A curious feature of the San Diego harbor until the 1940s was the log raft. Since there is little marketable timber in the immediate area, most lumber products used in building San Diego have had to be imported. In the very early period, entire buildings were brought around the Horn from Maine. Later, lumbermen began to bring logs twelve hundred miles from the Northwest in huge rafts. Some of the rafts were as much as nine hundred feet long, fifty to sixty feet wide, and thirty to forty feet deep. These rafts belonged to the Benson Lumber Company. Photograph courtesy of the San Diego Historical Society—Ticor Collection

One of the major projects during the Depression was the improvement of the harbor and waterfront. Financed by the WPA and other funds, Harbor Drive was improved, dredging was undertaken and the tidelands extended. A major part of that port improvement was the extension of the Broadway Pier (center of photograph) by two hundred feet and the building of a double-decked warehouse on it. With this addition, the pier was now one thousand feet long. Photograph courtesy of the San Diego Historical Society—Ticor Collection

Tuna canneries and packing houses were a common sight around the San Diego harbor in the 1930s. As the fishing industry expanded, so did the packing plants. The first, San Diego Packing Company, was built in 1914 at Point Loma. It opened with fifty employees but was eventually up to four hundred, mostly women, as seen in this 1935 photograph. In the 1930s, the tuna industry was at its peak, producing 100 million tons of fish per year. Photograph courtesy of the San Diego Historical Society—Ticor Collection

Although fishing has been a part of life around San Diego Bay since the first Indians arrived, *tuna* fishing did not become dominant until much later. Japanese fishermen introduced the use of poles to catch the fish. One of the leaders in the early tuna industry was Manuel O. Medina who came to San Diego in 1918; by 1939 the industry was catching 100 million pounds per year. These fishermen and their haul were probably photographed in the 1920s. Photograph courtesy of the San Diego Historical Society—Ticor Collection

As tuna fishing became more important to the area, local fishermen began to innovate. Beginning in the 1920s under leadership of Manuel O. Medina, tunamen began to build larger ships. The *Atlantic*, launched in 1931, is often called the first. It could carry up to one hundred tons of fish and could cruise up to three weeks and was so successful that it paid for itself in one year. The *Atlantic* generation of ships quickly became obsolete, however, as even larger ships were built, with four times the capacity and ocean ranges of up to several million square miles. This newer tuna clipper, the *Constitution*, even included a small seaplane for use in scouting for the tuna schools. Photograph courtesy of the Center for Regional History, San Diego State University

Not everyone in San Diego County was involved in work during the 1930s; there was some time for leisure. A new focus for that leisure was a turf club and racetrack in Del Mar. The track was on the Del Mar fairgrounds where a small WPA grant had made possible the construction of a grandstand. A clubhouse was added later with many Hollywood entertainment figures involved. One was Bing Crosby (shown on opening day, July 3, 1937, with Dorothy Lamour and some of the fifteen thousand others) who, with Pat O'Brien, loaned the racetrack several hundred thousand dollars to enable it to build the turf clubhouse. Photograph courtesy of the San Diego Historical Society—Ticor Collection

The dominant personality in San Diego aviation in the 1910s had been Glenn Curtiss; it was T. Claude Ryan and Charles Lindbergh in the 1920s; and it was Reuben H. Fleet in the 1930s. He was president of the Consolidated Aircraft Corporation, originally located in Buffalo, New York. After extensive research he decided that San Diego—with a good harbor, airport, sufficient labor supply, and the climate that would provide plenty of flying time—was the ideal location for his company. Accordingly, he moved his company to San Diego in 1935, guaranteeing San Diego a preeminent spot in the aviation industry, and giving a boost to the locality's recovery from the Depression. Photograph courtesy of the San Diego Historical Society—Ticor Collection

Reuben Fleet began his move to San Diego in 1935 and by January 15, 1937, the Consolidated Aircraft plant at Lindbergh Field was in place. Jeanne Rimmer recalls that Fleet paid the way for all employees who wanted to make the move from Buffalo to San Diego. She also remembers the move's impact on San Diego: "Having that aircraft plant come here, that was one of the main things that started to change San Diego just before the war. Because, you see, it gave a lot more employment to very skilled people. I remember my father coming home and talking about it [,] saying it was going to make a change." Two other major aircraft firms, Ryan and Solar, were also located on Lindbergh Field, and the fourth, Rohr, was in Chula Vista. Photograph courtesy of the San Diego Historical Society—Ticor Collection

As the rest of the world went to war in 1939, San Diego was, according to Richard Pourade, in *City of the Dream*, "the Navy's mightiest naval air base. . . . grouped around the shore of San Diego Bay were more than 600 government buildings representing an investment in buildings and equipment of more than $50,000,000." He further notes that thirty-two thousand Navy men called San Diego their home base. An example of the naval-air might was the first American aircraft carrier. The *Langley* docked in San Diego on July 3, 1939. Photograph courtesy of the San Diego Historical Society—Ticor Collection

The adoption of Consolidated Aircraft's vessels by major airlines, like United, guaranteed the company's and San Diego's prosperity. In 1939 one of the planes United had bought was christened *City of San Diego* with appropriate ceremony. The aircraft industry was so successful that by the end of the decade twenty thousand San Diegans were working in it, up from a few hundred in the 1920s. Photograph courtesy of the San Diego Historical Society—Ticor Collection

If anyone has any doubts about San Diego's status as a "Navy Town" in the thirties, note that the city's entry in the January 1, 1938 Rose Bowl Parade was in the form of a naval vessel and was headlined "Our Navy." Mayor Percy J. Benbough is following on horseback. Photograph courtesy of the San Diego Historical Society—Ticor Collection

Before getting down to war with Japan and Germany, San Diego had a smaller engagement to fight with the governor of California, Culbert Olson, and the city of Oakland. It was over a statue of Cabrillo by Alvaro De Bree which had been donated by Portugal in 1939 as a gift to California for the San Francisco World's Fair. It arrived too late and was placed in storage and promised by the governor to Oakland. State Senator Ed Fletcher of San Diego thought otherwise, and through bluff and chicanery, he and others "stole" the statue for San Diego. It was established on Harbor Island overlooking the Bay, and dedicated on December 19, 1940. Wartime security quickly made the statue inaccessible, and in 1959 it was moved to Cabrillo National Monument. Photograph courtesy of the Cabrillo National Monument

For many years San Diego citizens had turned down bond issues to build a civic center. Finally they passed one and in 1939 a building in modified Beaux Arts Mission Revival style was occupied. This photograph, which has clearly been touched up, apparently dates from 1939 and carried with it this contemporary caption: "The Building in the foreground is the $2,500,000 administration building which has been occupied since January, 1939. Planes shown above the city are a daily sight for our visitors and guests. San Diego is known as the 'Air Capital of the West' and it is here that the Navy maintains its largest air base." It is an appropriate statement upon which to conclude a consideration of the years before Pearl Harbor. Photograph courtesy of the California State Library

World War II and the military dominated San Diego from the beginning of the war until well into the 1950s. These sailors along Broadway in 1943 exemplify that. The war affected everything in the community—its economic development, housing, transportation, entertainment, and everyday life. And it continued long after the surrender of Japan. In *San Diego: Where California Began* (1976), Jim Mills points out that even in the 1950s, 78 percent of the income in San Diego was still generated—directly or indirectly—by the military. Photograph courtesy of the San Diego Historical Society—Ticor Collection

8

Wartime
Boomtowm

___

World War II brought to San
Diego a period of incredible
growth and a boomtime atmosphere. It
was a boom based on military spending;
one that lasted through the Korean
Conflict and into the Cold War. Indeed,
except for a brief sag after the Second
World War, San Diego has never really
ceased to be a wartime town. Not only
did the war and its aftermath accelerate
the growth and economy of the area, it
did much to give a special flavor to the
community. The war also laid the foundation for making San Diego a classic Sunbelt city in the period that followed.

As Maurice Tompkins has shown
in his master's thesis, "Military and
Civilian Aspects of San Diego During the
Second World War," the war affected the
city in almost every way possible. It
brought tremendous population growth,
with the city population going from

203,000 in 1940 to 334,000 in 1950; the population of the metropolitan area increased by an even larger percentage, going from 256,000 to 556,000. There was so much happening that as early as 1941, *Life Magazine* featured San Diego in a story titled "Boomtown: San Diego." In time, the *National Geographic* and *The Saturday Evening Post* also featured wartime San Diego.

The war brought an expansion of local military installations and the establishment of new ones. It brought thousands of soldiers to the area, plus their wives who stayed behind while the men went overseas. (The wives were often derisively called "Geraniums" by the locals). Thousands came through the city as they were processed in one of the training bases such as North Island, Marine Corps Recruit Depot, and Camp Callan. The war also brought huge defense manufacturing and service industries, the most important being aviation.

With the influx of the military and the growth of defense industries, the town was swamped. There was crowding and waiting in lines for everything. The most critical shortage was housing; one effort to solve that was the largest federal defense housing project in the country, the Linda Vista project. In addition there were transportation problems (ridership on the public transit facilities reached 375,000 per day at the peak of the war). The schools were overcrowded, crime increased, and there was continual discrimination against non-whites. The Japanese-Americans, of course, were removed from the area and sent to inland detention camps.

The community also had to deal with the special problems of World War II. One was the blackout. Especially after Pearl Harbor and several coastal scares, detailed plans were made to eliminate lights which would guide enemy planes to their target. There were civilian enforcement committees, which educated the population on proper lighting procedures, and saw to the enforcement of blackout regulations. A. I. Benedict of the Civilian Defense Office conducted correspondence with commercial enterprises and supervised much of the enforcement. You would be warned, one resident noted, if your venetian blinds were turned the wrong way (which let light out). There also were shortages of many foods, soaps, gasoline and tires, and many other goods. This led to the rationing system, which involved classifying people according to their needs, issuing ration books, and then having the distributors of goods obtain, record, and report stamps received for the rationed items. Some companies—the Klauber Wangenheim wholesale grocers, for example—had to add additional staff to handle the paperwork. It also led to bartering and a black market in many goods.

The war also shaped the social life of San Diego. It brought an influx of bars, movies, and a large outflux of sailors to Tijuana which sustained a considerable reputation in this period as a "sin city." The war also brought efforts by the civilian population to help the many service men in the city, as churches, clubs, and other organizations tried to help. The war also brought to town the "big bands" of the era who played for civilian and sailor alike in one of several large ballrooms.

World War II also brought to San Diego some permanent changes in the structure of its government. In 1943 the city established a planning commission with people from government, business, and the utilities to work together to plan for the present and future. It was the real beginning of planning for the community. Learning that at least 75 percent of those who were brought to the city by the war planned to stay afterwards, the city also hired a Philadelphia firm, Day and Zimmerman, to develop a master plan. This new planning activity eventually led to the development of the Cedar Street Mall idea in 1949, which would have grouped all public buildings together along Cedar Street. Like the previous Nolen Plans, nothing came of it. The city

As the war came closer, the United States government began to build up the military bases in San Diego. The process sharply accelerated after Pearl Harbor. In a short time established bases—such as the Naval Training Center shown here—were expanded with additional wooden and stucco buildings which increased capacity to thirty-three thousand trainees at one time. Other facilities were added—Camp Pendleton for the Marines; the Amphibious Training Base in Coronado; the Naval Air Station, Miramar; Gillespie Field, built for parachute training; and Brown Field, built near Imperial Beach. The harbor was improved and docking space for cruisers was added. Radar units were increased from six installations to seventy-five. Note also the warships in the harbor. As early as 1939 there were nearly three hundred Navy ships stationed here. Photograph courtesy of the San Diego Historical Society—Ticor Collection

did move, after the war, to develop one of its crown jewels, Mission Bay Park.

When the Second World War ended in August of 1945, there was great rejoicing in the streets—as there was all over the world. The town suffered a brief sag, with the immediate loss of thirty thousand jobs and about eighty thousand population. The setback was brief, however. The renewal of conflict with the Cold War led to continued high level of military readiness, the continued production of military armaments and supplies, all of which kept the San Diego economy roaring. In addition, as the space age emerged, the San Diego aviation industry became the aerospace industry as many of the rockets and missiles and components of the space age were manufactured here. Even as late as the 1950s, James Mills reports that 78 percent of San Diego's income was—directly or indirectly—from military sources. Only in the 1960s when there was some considerable shifting in military and related spending patterns did San Diego undergo a real postwar slump.

The wars—World War II, the Cold War, and the Korean—brought growth and prosperity to San Diego for almost two decades. They also brought changes in the nature of the community. Those changes, however, would be accelerated in the next decades, and with other factors, would make San Diego in the postwar years the essential Sunbelt city.

Although military construction in San Diego was extensive in the 1930s and early 1940s, defense installations were still somewhat limited. There was some improvement in 1940 with a modernization of batteries at Fort Rosecrans, which included cannon with a 25-mile range; eight-inch guns, ninety-millimeter antiaircraft batteries, and two sixteen-inch batteries. One of the sixteen-inch guns was at Ashburn Battery; it is not clear whether the woman is part of the defense installation or is merely practicing her Betty Grable imitation. (Actually she is posing after the war when the guns were being dismantled and melted down). Photograph courtesy of the Cabrillo National Monument

Not all the wartime planning and development was done by the military. As early as 1940 a civil defense system was being developed in meetings like this one. They worked on a civilian system of spotters, wardens, and blackout enforcers, and developed emergency plans for medical care, evacuation, and related problems. Their records at the San Diego Historical Society show that they developed means for dimming or reducing light output for all kinds of lights, carried on correspondence and inspections about blackouts, and similar activities. Photograph courtesy of the San Diego Historical Society— Ticor Collection

The major army installation in the area was the 1,162-acre Camp Callan on Torrey Pines Mesa. It opened in 1941 and before deactivation in December of 1945, it trained over 100,000 soldiers in a variety of enterprises. The first photograph shows troops arriving from Florida for training. Apparently they were expected to carry their own coathangers with them! The other picture shows soldiers engaged in a training exercise on the cliffs within the base—an area now occupied by the Torrey Pines Golf Course. Both photographs courtesy of the San Diego Historical Society—Ticor Collection

Yet another army base in San Diego County was Camp Lockett, established in 1941 near Campo on the Mexican border. Mounted troops trained there were used to patrol the border and to guard the water facilities at lakes Morena, Otay and Barrett. As the war progressed, water became an increasing problem for the city—civilian and military—and it was essential those facilities be secured. Photograph courtesy of the San Diego Historical Society—Ticor Collection

As soon as the bombing of Pearl Harbor became known, Americans of all walks of life began to throw themselves into the war effort. Apparently this included Americans of Japanese extraction. H. K. Morishita and K. Goto are shown on January 2, 1942, working on a poster advertising the "Free Japanese Committee to Aid Democracy." Their participation—and that of other West Coast residents with Japanese names—was quickly curtailed. Even before the war, there had been severe racial prejudice on the West Coast; after the attack on Hawaii, the fear that the Japanese represented a threat to American security became hysterical. Mexico moved its Japanese inland, as did Canada. In the United States both public and private groups and the United States military campaigned to remove the Japanese from the Pacific Coast. In San Diego County many groups—the County Board of Supervisors, Fallbrook Grange, La Mesa City Council, goaded by the editorials in the *San Diego Union*—campaigned for Japanese relocation. Finally it came with Executive Order No. 9066 on February 19, 1942, which led to the removal of 110,000 Japanese to inland detention camps. Photograph courtesy of the San Diego Historical Society—Ticor Collection

The program to deport Japanese from the coast hit San Diego hard. According to the Executive Order No. 4 of April 1, 1942, all Japanese—citizens and aliens alike—were to be "excluded" from the area south of the San Diego River by April 8, 1942. As a result, 1,150 San Diegans—like this family, properly tagged and ready for removal—were sent to the Santa Anita Race Track for processing, and then one of the bleak detention camps scattered throughout the inland West. Photograph courtesy of Donald Estes

Aside from the disruption of families, the shattering of friendships, and the violation of constitutional rights, the deported Japanese suffered tremendous financial loss. They had six days in which to dispose of their businesses, homes, personal property—everything except what they could carry on their backs or in a suitcase. Although many non-Japanese friends and neighbors arranged to buy things at a reasonable price, or to look after the deportees' interests while they were gone, most of the Japanese were forced to sell at frightfully low prices. Most were wiped out financially and after the war had to start over from scratch. Photograph courtesy of Donald Estes

"No loyal citizen of the United States should be denied the democratic right to exercise the responsibilities of his citizenship, regardless of his ancestry.

"The principle on which this country was founded and by which it has always been governed is that Americanism is a matter of the mind and heart.

"Americanism is not, and never was, a matter of race or ancestry.

"Every loyal American citizen should be given the opportunity to serve this country wherever his skills will make the greatest contribution—whether it be in the ranks of our armed forces, war production, agriculture, government service, or other work essential to the war effort."

THE PRESIDENT OF THE UNITED STATES, FEBRUARY 3, 1943

The justice of the internment of the Japanese during the war is still being debated. Justified at the time as a war measure to protect the security of the country, the action nonetheless clashed even then with such sentiments as President Roosevelt's statement in this 1943 poster: "Americanism is not, and never was, a matter of race or ancestry." Photograph courtesy of the San Diego Historical Society Research Archives

A unique and little-known part of San Diego's Second World War experience was the Yacht Patrol fleet. The "Yippees," or "YPs," were tuna boats such as the *Oceana* sequestered by the Navy and used for patrol and supply purposes throughout the Pacific—Panama, Samoa, Pearl Harbor, Guadalcanal, and many other places. Often their crew went with them, especially men from the local Portuguese community, which has great pride in their contribution to the war effort. After the war, Adm. William Haley Rogers credited them thusly: "They saved lives; and, they lost lives. Then, as always, they served their country well." Photograph courtesy of the Center for Regional History, San Diego State University

Although the city was a huge military base, it must be remembered that the manufacturing of war goods was the major occupation of those living in San Diego during the war. San Diegans manufactured many kinds of war goods, but mostly they built things associated with aviation—airplane components, equipment, parachutes, and the airplanes themselves. The largest manufacturer of airplanes was Convair (formerly Consolidated Aircraft), which built 30,900 airplanes between July 1, 1940, and August 31, 1945, making it second among airplane manufactuers in the nation. One of the planes they built in San Diego was the PBY patrol bomber (of which 3,000 were built) shown here in San Diego. Convair also built over 6,700 B-24 Liberator bombers in its Lindbergh Field plants. Photograph courtesy of the San Diego Historical Society—Ticor Collection

Workers are on the way to their jobs at Convair on April 15, 1943; note the camouflage net covering the entire complex. The labor force for wartime San Diego came from all over. It included women, Afro-Americans (usually in less skilled jobs), Mexicans, and a large number of "Oakies" who had left Oklahoma and Arkansas in the 1930s. Recruiting and maintaining an adequate labor force for the defense and service industries was a severe problem throughout the war, and San Diego concerns ranged as far away as Minnesota to Texas to find workers. Photograph courtesy of the San Diego Historical Society—Ticor Collection

Shipment March 2/43   136 Field Boxes   5440 pounds Avocados

Another important contribution of the San Diego area to the war effort was agriculture. One local crop was avocado, as shown by these 5,400 pounds of avocados harvested on March 2, 1943. Much of the labor for the care and harvesting of agricultural crops was Mexican. Prior to this time most Mexican immigrants coming to the area had bypassed San Diego for Los Angeles, but that changed somewhat during the war, and more stayed in the region. The percentage of the county's population which was Hispanic increased from 3.1 percent in 1940 to 4.6 percent in 1946. Photograph courtesy of the San Diego Historical Society—Ticor Collection

One of the worst shortages civilian San Diegans experienced during the war was housing. A number of solutions were offered; the largest was a government project to build a huge complex on Linda Vista Mesa. It was the largest defense housing project in the country and was started on March 5, 1941. The plans called for building enough homes in three hundred days to house thirteen thousand people. Although 255 units were finished in thirty days, problems arose and progress dragged after that. There were no schools, no fire and police protection, and the plans for a shopping center had been dropped for lack of funding. Because of poor planning, the entire water supply for thirteen thousand people came through one ten-inch water main. But the project was finished and did help; it was also a pioneering effort in government housing. Photograph courtesy of the San Diego Historical Society—Ticor Collection

As the war got underway the sheer number of people to be moved, coupled with gasoline and rubber shortages, forced heavy use of the public transit system—streetcars and buses. By 1943, 375,000 per day were riding the system. Eighty percent of the ridership was connected with the war effort in a direct way. This heavy use of public transportation led to another shortage—personnel to run the system. Recruiting efforts were made as far east as the Mississippi River, and local recruiting activities included such stunts as this. Photograph courtesy of the San Diego Historical Society Public Library Collection

Much of the demand for transportation personnel was met by women. By 1943 the bus company was using over one hundred women as drivers, with another eight hundred as mechanics, receivers, or clerks. Other women like Ada Miller, Gravine Linville, Frances Prescott, Ethel Baker, and Hilda Ryan drove taxicabs. Despite their best efforts, the taxi shortage was still terrible. If you wanted to catch a four o'clock airplane, you had to call the cab early in the morning. Photograph courtesy of the San Diego Historical Society—Ticor Collection

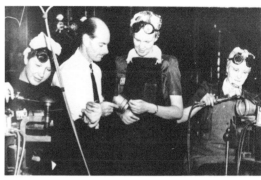

Women also worked in the defense plants; in fact in San Diego eventually 40 percent of the defense jobs were held by women. In order to both recruit women and to erode some of the prejudice of women doing jobs that had previously been identified as male jobs, educational exhibits such as this were set up in a number of downtown department store windows. In this window at Walker's Department Store, a woman is demonstrating how to bend tubing. The next picture, from the trade publication, *Solar Blast* shows that the educational programs must have been effective. Vivian Haktsian, Emily Christiansen and Madilyn Bledsoe were the first welders to work for Solar. They are seen with their foreman, George Bradley. Photographs courtesy of the San Diego Historical Society—Ticor Collection and *Solar Blast* (November, 1952)

The black population of San Diego increased somewhat during the war, but little else changed. White prejudice kept Afro-Americans primarily in unskilled jobs as domestic workers, janitors, or laborers. By 1944, about thirty-two hundred worked in defense industries or for the government, and another two thousand in service industries. In addition to job discrimination (despite President Franklin Roosevelt's Executive Order No. 8802 prohibiting racial discrimination in defense industries), black San Diegans were also discriminated against in housing and transportation and by the entertainment industries. As indicated in this 1945 picket line at the New Victory movie house in Imperial Beach, not all Afro-Americans were willing to accept the continuation of that discrimination. Photograph courtesy of the San Diego Historical Society—Ticor Collection

The Chinese were in a special position during the war. They had a unique problem in that many whites confused them with the Japanese; on the other hand they had a favored status in that their motherland, China, was an ally in the Pacific War. They worked hard for the war effort, as illustrated by this float on a La Jolla street in 1945. It is surrounded with American red, white, and blue bunting, and is advertising a program to benefit the China war relief program. Photograph courtesy of the San Diego Historical Society—Ticor Collection

San Diego civilians contributed to the war effort in many ways. For example, in advertising its Point Loma brand of canned goods, the Klauber Wangenheim Company exhorted the community to "Plant your Victory Garden," and to help them feed the city. This particular billboard ran in February and March 1943. Photograph courtesy of the Klauber Wangenheim Company

BARGE AHEAD WITH WAR BONDS!

Buy an EXTRA $100 in the 4TH WAR LOAN

San Diego County War Finance Committee

WANTED!

FOR MURDER

Her careless talk costs lives

Do with less—so they'll have enough!

RATIONING GIVES YOU YOUR FAIR SHARE

YOUR BLOOD CAN SAVE HIM

RED CROSS MOBILE UNIT

WHITMAN

The civilian population was constantly being exhorted by posters to do its part in the war effort. Many were used during the war; some were of local origin and others were national.

These samples, photographed by Ken Jacques from the San Diego Historical Society collection, are typical. They urge the citizenry to buy bonds, to conserve food, to donate blood, and

to keep quiet. Posters courtesy of the San Diego Historical Society Research Archives

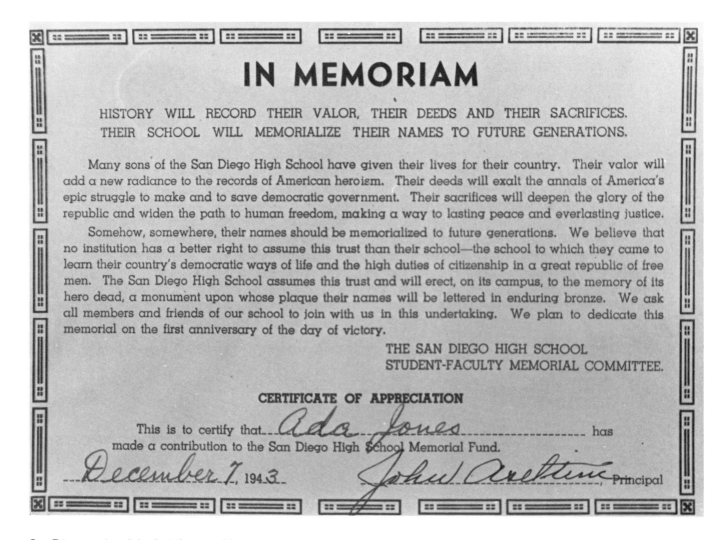

IN MEMORIAM

HISTORY WILL RECORD THEIR VALOR, THEIR DEEDS AND THEIR SACRIFICES. THEIR SCHOOL WILL MEMORIALIZE THEIR NAMES TO FUTURE GENERATIONS.

Many sons of the San Diego High School have given their lives for their country. Their valor will add a new radiance to the records of American heroism. Their deeds will exalt the annals of America's epic struggle to make and to save democratic government. Their sacrifices will deepen the glory of the republic and widen the path to human freedom, making a way to lasting peace and everlasting justice.

Somehow, somewhere, their names should be memorialized to future generations. We believe that no institution has a better right to assume this trust than their school—the school to which they came to learn their country's democratic ways of life and the high duties of citizenship in a great republic of free men. The San Diego High School assumes this trust and will erect, on its campus, to the memory of its hero dead, a monument upon whose plaque their names will be lettered in enduring bronze. We ask all members and friends of our school to join with us in this undertaking. We plan to dedicate this memorial on the first anniversary of the day of victory.

THE SAN DIEGO HIGH SCHOOL
STUDENT-FACULTY MEMORIAL COMMITTEE.

CERTIFICATE OF APPRECIATION

This is to certify that _Ada Jones_ has made a contribution to the San Diego High School Memorial Fund.

December 7, 1943　　　_John Aseltine_, Principal

San Diegans also did what they could to remember those who fell overseas. One effort was by San Diego High School which decided to erect a monument on the high school grounds listing all from the school who died in the conflict. This December 7, 1943 certificate indicates that Ada Jones had made a contribution to that monument. It is signed by Dr. John Aseltine, long-time and highly regarded principal of San Diego High School. Photograph courtesy of the San Diego High School Alumni Association

Many people volunteered for a variety of tasks during the war period. These women in the Red Cross are learning how to use gas masks. Others volunteered for the USO, as air raid captains, to lead paper and scrap metal drives, to sell bonds, and in a variety of other programs. It is assumed that such volunteer work helped keep civilian morale high

during the war. Photograph courtesy of the San Diego Historical Society— Ticor Collection

Entertaining the thousands of sailors and the hundreds of thousands of San Diego residents was a special problem. It was met in many ways, several of which are illustrated here: Some went to burlesque shows, such as the "Big Girl Revue" in 1943. Others visited bars, such as the "Bomber" as of April 10, 1943. One English writer said about San Diego that it "was a great naval port with a bar on every street corner and several dozen sailors in every bar." Some may have thought they were teenagers back home, like these young army men at the drugstore fountain on base at Camp Callan. All three photographs courtesy of the San Diego Historical Society—Ticor Collection

As a large training center for both the Army and the Navy, San Diego was the scene of many troop movements. This troop ship, on the Broadway pier, was entertained by the Marine Depot Band led by Drum Majorette Marion Caster (left of center) who had been majorette at San Diego High School and San Diego State College, and was probably the model for the neon artwork on the Campus Theatre on El Cajon Boulevard. Photograph courtesy of Marion Caster Baker

The war is over. With the Japanese surrender on August 14, 1945, San Diego joined much of the rest of the world in a wild spontaneous celebration filled with joy. Photograph courtesy of the San Diego Historical Society—Ticor Collection

The end of the war also was a time of
tears—tears of parting, tears of joy?
Photograph courtesy of the San
Diego Historical Society—Ticor
Collection

When World II ended, many thought San Diego could collapse. Military installations and defense industries began to shut down fast. Convair went from forty-four thousand employees to fourteen thousand in 1945; Ryan fell from eighty-five hundred to two thousand. Over eighty thousand people deserted the town in 1945. It was to this downturn that the soldiers returned. Their problem is illustrated by this 1946 protest by unemployed veterans. The problems was short lived, however, as 75 percent of the World War II newcomers to San Diego stayed, and the tensions of the Cold War and the Korean Conflict brought San Diego renewed growth.

WE ARE STILL FIGHTING 1946

ATOM BOMB

FOX HOLE 1946 STYLE

9

A Sunbelt City: San Diego 1945-1972

—

The Second World War brought many changes to the United States—and few were as significant as the shift in population and power from the North and East to the South and Southwest. The area of growth became known as the Sunbelt. People were drawn to the Sunbelt because of jobs created by continued government military and defense spending, by a good business climate, and by a high quality of life with good educational opportunities, recreational facilities, newer and nicer housing, and better weather. If one uses the characteristics of a Sunbelt city as set out in Richard Bernard and Bradley Rice, *Sunbelt Cities: Politics and Growth Since World War II* (1983), San Diego is the almost perfect example of a Sunbelt city. After the war, San Diego experienced phenomenal population growth as the metropolitan area went from

When World War II ended, San Diego's metropolitan area had a population of nearly 500,000. Although San Diego was a large city in terms of population, this 1950 photograph of the skyline—looking up Broadway—shows that its appearance was still that of the 1930s. The tallest buildings in 1950 were still the Bank of America and the El Cortez Hotel, and the two large U.S. Navy structures still dominate the waterfront. Note that some temporary war buildings can still be seen in the right front of the picture. In many ways, San Diego's emergence as a real city was yet to come. Photograph courtesy of the San Diego Historical Society—Ticor Collection

256,368 in 1940 to 1,357,854 in 1970. The local economy was stimulated by defense and other government spending. The "quality of life" was unexcelled, and the limited unionization of the labor force and the business-dominated political structure created a "good business climate." San Diego 1945-1972 was the quintessential Sunbelt City.

Military and defense spending shaped San Diego's great growth in the generation after the Second World War. Although both seemed headed for a shutdown with V-J Day in 1945, the Cold War and Korea, coupled with the space race, quickly brought the military and the aerospace industry back into full bloom in San Diego. Throughout most of the period, about one-fourth of the people of San Diego worked for the United States Navy, and one-sixth worked in the aerospace industry. They produced civilian and military airplanes, missiles, rockets, and weapons components. In addition to the military and defense industries, other parts of the economy prospered. The port was improved and exported the Imperial Valley's agricultural goods in great quantity. With the development of better technology and fishing methods, the tuna fishing industry grew and remained strong into the 1970s. The limited but highly-specialized agricultural enterprises prospered, and the percentage of service industries in the economy began to climb. Another major and growing industry was tourism, which was moving up the economic ladder.

In this time, the economy received a major boost, strangely enough, from an economic disaster. In the early 1960s there was a sharp decline in federal defense and aerospace spending. Furthermore, Convair, which had been a locally controlled firm, was taken over by General Dynamics. To make matters worse, its commercial aircraft were not selling. Between 1960 and 1962, aerospace jobs in San Diego dropped 20 percent, Convair went from twenty-two thousand jobs to six thousand and racked up a one-billion-dollar deficit, the largest ever for a corporation up to that time. San Diego, the "Boomtown" became known in the national press as San Diego, the "Doomtown." Spurred by this, the city struck back aggressively.

In typical Sunbelt city manner, much of San Diego's postwar growth and prosperity was the result of government spending—either for the military or for defense industries. With the Cold War and continued military tensions in the 1950s and 1960s, San Diego continued to be a major aviation manufacturing center. As one commentator, Neal R. Pierce, put it, the Cold War "really saved San Diego from the ravishes of peace." The major employer continued to be Convair (eventually absorbed by General Dynamics), shown here (upper right) manufacturing airplanes for the United States Airforce. Smaller firms, such as Ryan, Rohr, and Solar remained important—Solar continued to specialize in highly intricate research and manufacturing of very sensitive components. The photograph above shows them testing afterburners for military jet engines. In addition to aircraft, San Diego industries were also active in the space program. For instance, when John Glenn became the first man to circle the globe, he was lifted off the ground in an Atlas rocket made in San Diego. Photographs courtesy of *Solar Blast* (November, 1952) and San Diego State University Archives

While the military, aerospace, and tourism dominated San Diego's phenomenal growth after the Second World War, shipping and the commercial harbor still continued to be important. In order to tap the growing production of agricultural goods from the Imperial Valley, San Diego opened the Tenth Street Terminal in 1958. By that time, the city had already shipped out the one millionth bale of Imperial Valley/Mexicali cotton. In 1960 over $1 million was spent to improve grain and bulk loading facilities, and in the 1970s the expanded facilities at the Twenty-fourth Street Terminal in National City (see photograph) were opened. This new terminal gave San Diego the largest marine terminal on the West Coast. Photograph courtesy of the San Diego State University Archives

It organized an Economic Development Corporation (EDC) to bring in new and diversified industries. It saw the horrible example of Los Angeles and its pollution, so the EDC focused its efforts on clean, non-polluting "high-tech" industries and services. Such industries would complement its educational, research and aerospace industries, as well. The EDC developed an industrial park, and priviate interests developed fifteen more. Many new companies—Cubec, Wavetek, National Cash Register, Hewlett-Packard, Sony, Burroughs, and Hughes Tools, for example—came to town. These new industries, coupled with growing research facilities, set San Diego on the direction to both a more diversified economy and a role as a major center of high-tech industry.

At the same time San Diego made a conscious decision to stress the visitor industry. Perhaps remembering former mayor Edwin Capps's comment that tourists did not disturb the geraniums, "and when they departed no smoke-stacks were left behind, only money," the city pushed its tourist assets—the San Diego Zoo, Balboa Park, Sea World, Cabrillo National Monument, its proximity to Mexico, and its climate—to attract visitors. The industry has grown to the point that by the mid-1980s, it employs eighty-three thousand San Diegans, and attracts twenty-nine million visitors who spend $2,250,000,000 per year.

While trying to diversify the economy, the city leaders, in this case organized as "San Diegans, Inc.," also made an effort to revive the downtown, which had been killed by the growth of freeways and shopping centers. The efforts of the community led to the construction of private office buildings and hotels downtown, and the creation of a city civic center with public buildings and a major auditorium.

That sick downtown was mostly the result of one of the major developments in San Diego, 1945-1972: the freeway system and its accompaniments. The first freeway opened in 1948, and

within a generation, there were over 250 miles of urban freeways. The freeway made possible a dispersal of the population out of the old city area into widely-scattered, low-density suburbs. In the 1950s developers opened areas around State College, in Del Cerro, Serra Mesa, Mission Village, Allied Gardens, and Clairemont. In the next decade the city moved into University City, San Carlos, Lake Murray, and small cities on the outer edges of San Diego. La Mesa, El Cajon, National City, and Chula Vista experienced rapid growth.

The freeway-suburban world also made possible the regional shopping center. Beginning in 1960 with College Grove, Mission Valley and Grossmont, large department stores and specialty shops moved out of downtown and into the regional centers. The shopping centers helped spawn a new and informal way of life with their easy and abundant parking, quick access and casual atmosphere. Along with drive-in movies and restaurants, drag races and "cruising," they helped shape San Diego into an automobile-dominated city. Or to be more precise, San Diego became a collection of suburbs looking for a city.

While growing in size and numbers, San Diego was also growing in public facilities. The aquatic park, Mission Bay, was dedicated in 1949. It involved the remaking of False Bay into a dream park of beaches, boating, fishing, hotels, and other water-oriented recreational facilities. The city also built the aforementioned civic theatre and exposition facilities downtown, plus a new (if already outdated) public library building. Another indication of the suburban nature of the city's growth is that while building a new central library downtown, the city also built a large number of branch libraries to serve all of the new suburbs. The state also built in this period a new bridge connecting Coronado with the city center. This was deemed necessary to serve the large working force at the Naval Air Station on North Island. Just as the freeway system and auto-

Another industry which remained important was tuna fishing. From the end of the Second World War into the 1970s, there were over two hundred long-distance fishing vessels based in San Diego, along with ship building and repair yards, and packing and canning establishments. One reason the industry prospered after the war was the increase in the size of ships (from an average crew of eight to an average of twenty), more refrigeration, better radio systems, radar for locating the fish, and most-important, the introduction of purse seining. This involved using a large net with cork floats on top and weights on the bottom. A power skiff encircled a school of fish with the net, and the bottom was closed (i.e., "pursed") and machinery lifted the huge fish-filled nets into the boat. It was a great improvement over the old pole-fishing method and tunamen converted to the new system within a couple of years. This 1948 photograph shows the *General McArthur* [sic] "hauling around" a school of fish off Costa Rica. Photograph courtesy of the Center for Regional History, San Diego State University

San Diego suffered its 1950s Red Scare-McCarthyism casualty. Harry C. Steinmetz, a psychology teacher at San Diego State College, was removed from his post by the State Board of Education in 1954 when he refused to tell state authorities whether he was ever a communist. The incident was upheld by the State Supreme Court, and the United States Supreme Court refused to hear the case. Although Steinmetz tried several times to obtain restitution, none had been forthcoming by his death in 1981. Steinmetz had long been one of San Diego's more colorful figures, having been president of the Trade Council in the 1930s, and having run for mayor on a Socialist ticket. He had also been a longtime aggressive pacificist. A representative of leftist politics, Steinmetz won few victories in the extremely-conservative, usually-Republican San Diego political arena. Photograph courtesy of the San Diego State University Archives

mobile killed the streetcar system (the last car ran in 1949); the Coronado Bridge killed the romantic ferry system which had connected Coronado with San Diego since the 1880s.

In its move to become a major city, San Diego spent $28 million to build a major sports stadium in the flood plain of the San Diego River. It was built to house the American Football League team, the San Diego Chargers; and the San Diego State College Aztecs, who, with "Air Coryell," were setting national records with their passing attack. In time the city also acquired an expansion baseball team, the Padres. It was so poor in the beginning that San Diegans asked for years after its appearance: "When will professional baseball ever come to San Diego?" San Diego also acquired an indoor sports arena, but was not successful in holding on to professional basketball and hockey teams.

Another growth industry of the era was higher education. When World War II ended, San Diego had one college, San Diego State College, a nice little liberal arts school. By the end of the period, San Diego State College had become San Diego State University. It was one of the larger metropolitan universities in the nation and was beginning to attract national attention. Two new church-related institutions—California Western College on Point Loma, and the University of San Diego, a Roman Catholic institution in Alcala Park—entered the scene. In 1964 the University of California, which already had the world-famous Scripps Institution of Oceanography, opened the doors of a branch in La Jolla. The University of California campus focused on science, medicine and research; it quickly became one of the most prestigious science-oriented universities in the nation. Thousands of other San Diegans attended a rapidly expanding network of junior colleges, which were being renamed "community colleges." This educational system formed the base for the city's growth as a research and high-tech

center which, by the 1980s, had the highest level of education of any major metropolitan center in the country.

San Diego also created new cultural institutions in the postwar generation. The Timken Gallery of traditional paintings opened in 1965 in Balboa Park—in a very modernistic building. Under the leadership of Bea Evenson, the city rebuilt the Casa Del Prado to preserve the baroque Spanish architectural style of the 1915 exposition. The Rueben Fleet Space Theatre opened in a nice Hispanic building in 1973. The Mexican-American cultural influence on the city was recognized when the Centro Cultural de la Raza opened in 1971 as an art center located in an old water tank in Balboa Park. At the universities, further recognition was granted to some of the non-white population when courses and programs were introduced in Afro-American, Mexican-American, and American Indian Studies. At the University of California, one whole college was devoted to third world cultures.

The San Diego Zoo continued to hold its place in the forefront of zoos. Charles Schroeder, its director 1952-1972, professionalized the zoo's operations and made two major innovations. He created the Children's Zoo, which allowed visitors and animals to mingle together in some of the exhibits. This was so successful that the concept was extended to a number of exhibits in the main zoo. Schroeder was also responsible for creation of the Wild Animal Park north of the city. It was conceived originally as a site for breeding and preservation of endangered species, but gradually the zoo came to realize that the Wild Animal Park had educational and recreational possibilities as well. Thus a monorail was built around the large exhibit areas, which allowed visitors to see the animals in a realistic and natural setting. The Wild Animal Park was hailed as the zoo of the future.

Politically San Diego typified the Sunbelt pattern in that the downtown business elite dominated its politics. The

Few things have changed San Diego as much as freeways. The first was the Cabrillo Freeway through Balboa Park, which connected downtown with Mission Valley. It was built in 1948 after much opposition (the highway department planted 500,000 trees along its route to mollify the angry natives). Others followed almost immediately, and by 1983 there was over 250 miles of freeway in the metropolitan area. This allowed construction of large regional shopping centers, extension of the city via low-density suburbs, and all but killed downtown. This 1951 photograph shows the intersection of Cabrillo Freeway with Interstate 8, which is the major east-west automobile route in the area. Within a decade the cultivated areas seen in this photograph began to fill with a shopping center, hotels and commercial buildings. Photograph courtesy of the San Diego Historical Society—Ticor Collection

overall tone of San Diego politics was very conservative, with some Red Scare-McCarthyism activities and some active members of the John Birch Society. A key feature of the local conservativism was the hostility to federal aid, which caused the city to eschew federal money for urban renewal, downtown development and many other projects. The conservative political climate also worked against effective planning and controlled development, which led to some decisions which are now seen as major mistakes. Racial and ethnic minorities remained outside the mainstream of political life, as they have been since the Anglo-American takeover of the city in 1846. This occurred despite the fact that 14.8 percent of the population in 1970 was Hispanic and 5.6 percent was Afro-American.

The quarter century after World War II saw this Sunbelt city grow in size, space, population and public institutions. The town was so concerned with growth in quantity that it did not always think very much about quality. By the end of the period San Diego was clearly a larger city, but still something of a drab one. That would change in the next period of the city's history, the era of "America's Finest City."

The freeway system ushered in a new era and dealt a death blow to an old one, the streetcar era. The streetcar system had served the city well for over half a century; indeed during World War II, it had carried as many as 375,000 passengers a day. By 1949, the system was abandoned and the last car, "Old 446" was "Retired With Honor For a Job Well Done!" In the late 1970s, when a new trolley system was inaugurated, it was regarded as an innovation in public transportation! Photograph courtesy of the San Diego Historical Society Public Library Collection

As San Diego sprawled out over the countryside, the freeway and suburban subdivision were joined by the shopping center to create a new way of life. Beginning with the opening of this center, College Grove, in 1960, regional shopping centers appeared along most of the major freeways. Other early ones were Mission Valley (built in opposition to the city staff and in blatant disregard for the flooding likely to occur in a river bottom), and Grossmont in the eastern part of the city. Most major downtown department and specialty shops established branches in the shopping centers; in time they closed their downtown establishments and downtown died as a shopping area. Ironically, the core of the 1980s revival of downtown is still another shopping center—Horton Plaza—located in the center of the city. Photograph courtesy of the San Diego Historical Society—Ticor Collection

These two aerial photographs of the San Diego State College area, taken in 1934 and 1953, illustrate the nature and extent of San Diego's post-war suburban growth. As can be noted by focusing on College and Montezuma streets, most of the land on top of the mesas was settled after 1934 by low-density, one-family dwellings. If there were apartments, they were landscaped garden apartments, usually with swimming pool. The growth here was comparable to that occurring in Clairemont, Allied Gardens, Del Cerro, and Serra Mesa at the same time. In the next decade University City, San Carlos, and Lake Murray were created, and suburban towns such as La Mesa, El Cajon, and Chula Vista experienced similar suburban expansion. Clearly the entire approach to growth depends upon the automobile and imported water. The low density of the settlement probably means that future public transportation will be difficult to develop, as there would be limited ridership per square mile. The suburban postwar growth in San Diego has probably shaped the city for the foreseeable future. Photographs courtesy of the San Diego Historical Society Public Library Collection

The automobile culture of postwar San Diego showed up in many ways. Survivors of the era will remember the introduction of drive-in grocery stores, liquor stores, cleaners, and most important of all, drive-in cafes and moving pictures. As an automobile town with a benign climate, San Diego had plenty of both. Oscars, shown in 1947, was the epitome of the drive-in restaurant which is now celebrated in television and cinema. Of the many drive-in movie theatres in San Diego, none is better remembered than the Campus, noted for its huge neon scene of San Diego State College and its Aztec drum majorette. The model was Marion Caster Baker, former majorette for San Diego High School and State College, who was seen earlier leading the Aztec band at the waterfront (see page 198). The neon artwork is considered a classic of its type and was featured in *Life* magazine. When the theater was torn down, the neon was preserved, to be reassembled at another site and in another time. Photographs courtesy of Jerry Hebert and San Diego Historical Society— Ticor Collection

Downtown San Diego declined steadily into the 1960s. When that decline was coupled with a sharp economic turndown (caused when Convair was merged with General Dynamics and went from twenty-two thousand jobs to six thousand with a corporate loss of $1 billion), San Diego business leaders were galvanized into action. They created an Economic Development Corporation to revitalize and diversify the economy. They focused on industrial parks for clean high-tech industries, tourism, and revitalization of downtown. One approach for downtown was to attract private buildings (banks, savings and loans,

corporate headquarters) and to create a downtown civic center. Previous efforts to build a civic center with bond issues had all failed, but this time the clever city manager, Thomas Fletcher, managed to use other sources and built a civic center including city offices, a small exposition center, a parking facility, concourse, and a major civic auditorium. All parts were open by 1965. This night view focuses on the civic center, with the auditorium in the center; it also shows some of the new private buildings being added to the skyline. Photograph courtesy of the San Diego State University Archives

The postwar years saw another jewel added to the city's crown, Mission Bay Park, which was dedicated in 1949. It was built on False Bay, which had been used for little more than duck hunting prior to this. Around 1930, City Planning Director Glenn C. Rick began to push the idea of making it a major aquatic park. Finally the state transferred the site to the city (which bought additional acreage, and, beginning soon after the war, the city and the United States Corps of Engineers began to shape the new park. They rerouted the San Diego River to keep silt out; dredged a new entrance, built a jetty, and dredged the bay to depths ranging from eight to twenty-two feet. As can be seen in the first photograph, the fill was used to create islands and beaches. By the late 1960s, over $70 million had been spent and over eighty-thousand visitors per day were enjoying the park on weekends. The park included hotels (the first was the Bahia opened in 1953), boating facilities, beaches, parks, and fishing for all ages (seen in the second photograph). Yet another attraction was Sea World, a research and entertainment center with an aquatic theme. It is still a favorite with locals and visitors alike. Photographs courtesy of the Center for Regional History, San Diego State University

One indication of San Diego's emergence as a major city during this period was the construction of a $28 million stadium and the attraction of professional sports. The new stadium housed the San Diego Chargers and San Diego State University football teams, who were joined in 1969 by a baseball team, the Padres. The stadium is shown here on June 1, 1967, while it was still under construction in the flood plain of the San Diego River; and again on May 31, 1968, when Bob Hope hosted a show to raise funds for the USO. Photographs courtesy of the Center for Regional History, San Diego State University

Coronado and North Island have always been hard to get to from San Diego; after the 1880s access was by ferryboat. With the high level of employment at the naval installations of North Island the traffic problem was critical and demands grew for a bridge over the bay. Coronado City Council began pushing in the early 1950s and finally the Navy let it be known they would have no objections to a bridge, so long as it provided a two-hundred-foot clearance for their ships. The result was the construction by the state of the Coronado Bridge, a 2.2 mile span, with a graceful ninety-degree curve and a spectacular view. It was opened in 1969. Photograph courtesy of the Center for Regional History, San Diego State University

Yet another example of San Diego's growing postwar role as a center of scientific research was the opening in 1948 of the Palomar Observatory in the mountains north of the city. It has a two-hundred-inch mirror lens which enables viewers to see stars one billion light years away. It is still the most powerful telescope in the United States. The first photograph shows the lens as it was being unloaded in 1948. Note the protective crate overhead; it has just been lifted off the well-wrapped lens. The second photograph shows the exterior of the observatory in its alpine setting. Photographs courtesy of San Diego Historical Society—Ticor Collection and the San Diego Convention and Visitors Bureau

A major growth industry in San Diego from 1945 to 1972 was higher education. San Diego State College (formed in 1897 as San Diego Normal School; soon to become San Diego State University) remained the largest as it grew to twenty-three thousand students by the 1970s. By the mid-1980s it enrolled over thirty-three thousand and was one of the largest urban universities in the country. Since the 1930s, when State moved to Montezuma Mesa, the Mission-Revival buildings have remained the core of the campus and have given the institution its identity. This photograph toward the end of this period shows the original buildings, but also shows (to the left) the new Drama Building, and much of the new landscaping which was just being developed. In this period, the growth of San Diego State was matched by the emergence of California Western College, the University of California, and the La Jolla branch of the University of California. Photograph courtesy of the San Diego State University Archives

While San Diego State was growing in size during the Sunbelt years, it was also growing in distinction. An indication of its emerging stature is illustrated by the fact that President John F. Kennedy gave the commencement address in 1963. President Kennedy is at the center of the photograph; San Diego State College President Malcolm A. Love is at the podium. During the years 1952 to 1971, Malcolm Love guided State through the transition from a small teachers' college to a major urban university. Despite San Diego's basically conservative political atmosphere, the university faculty and many former students still regard President Kennedy's visit as the high point of the university's history. Photograph courtesy of the San Diego State University Archives

This 1970 photograph says a lot about San Diego State College at the time. In the first place, it is a picture of a construction fence, a ubiquitous feature of the campus as it underwent physical expansion to accommodate its growing enrollments. This particular fence was around the library, which was itself larger than the entire campus when it opened at the Montezuma Mesa site in the 1930s. Other buildings added were for the social sciences, business and mathematics, chemistry and geology, a new gymnasium, and a student union. The other reason the photograph says a lot is because the slogans indicate the presence of the radicalism of the late 1960s and early 1970s. In the era of the Vietnam War, the fence exhorts the viewer to "Love;" and also urges the system to "Let Students Rule." San Diego State had limited radical demonstrations and activities on campus during those years of turmoil, but that turmoil did bring some permanent changes (see next photograph). Photograph courtesy of the San Diego State University Archives

A woman in a classroom might not seem like anything unusual; what makes this one noteworthy is that this woman is participating in a meeting in a Department of Women's Studies classroom. One effect of the radical 1960s and 1970s was change in American universities. Students were given a role in policy and personnel decisions; changes were made in curriculums; and in some cases, programs and departments were created to meet the needs of less-advantaged elements of society. At San Diego State, this involved the creation of departments of Afro-American Studies, Mexican-American Studies, American Indian Studies, and Women's Studies. All taught courses in their respective fields, provided positive role models, and worked with the community to recruit and retain students. At San Diego State the most successful has been the Women's Studies program, which was the first in the nation when it was created in 1970. It has been featured frequently in women's literature and is considered the strongest as well as the oldest in the country. Photograph courtesy of the San Diego State University Women's Studies Department

As part of the growth of postwar higher education, two small church-related institutions came into being. One was California Western College started on the site of Madame Tingley's Theosophical Institute on Point Loma. In time it emerged into United States International University, which moved to Scripps Ranch and several other campuses; their old site on Point Loma was then taken over by Point Loma Nazarene College. The other institution was the University of San Diego, which opened as a women's college, then added a men's college and a law school. The various operations were legally combined in 1972 to become the University of San Diego, a diocesan university. The photograph shows the campus under construction in 1948. As befits a church-related school (the bishop's chancery is on campus), the site is dominated by the magnificent church in the center of the picture. The entire campus has been built in a Hispanic style reminiscent of the 1915 Panama California Exposition; sitting atop a hill, the University of San Diego is one of the city's most striking complexes of buildings. Photograph courtesy of the San Diego Historical Society—Ticor Collection

La Jolla's Scripps Institution of Oceanography has been a maritime oriented research center of the University of California since early in the twentieth century. After the Second World War, one of its leaders, Roger Revelle, developed a dream of building a full-fledged campus around Scripps. He fought for his dream for years and in 1964 the first undergraduate began attending classes at the University of California, San Diego. The branch of the University of California is organized on a college basis, like Oxford, and focuses heavily on science and research. The center of the campus is the main library, which opened in 1970. It has a capacity for nearly two million books, and in 1985 ranked forty-first among United States and Canadian academic libraries. The

unique building was designed by William L. Pereira and is considered by many the most spectacular piece of architecture on the campus. Others think it looks like a flying saucer about to take off! Photograph courtesy of the University of California, San Diego

As part of its science-oriented educational and research facilities, San Diego has attracted a number of private institutions. An example is the Salk Institute. The institute was the brainchild of Dr. Jonas Salk, who developed in 1955 the first anti-polio vaccine. From the early 1950s he dreamed of a research facility to work on problems of life and health. His dream came true when the city of San Diego ceded him land near the University of California's new campus, and the March of Dimes (National Foundation for Infantile Paralysis) pledged $20 million to construct such a center. Housed in a highly-praised building designed by Louis Kahn, the institute opened in 1965. It has become a major health-

related research organization, working on such problems as cancer, diabetes, multiple sclerosis, and the immune system. Jonas Salk has be-

come one of San Diego's most-revered citizens. Photograph courtesy of the San Diego Historical Society—Ticor Collection

Whale watching is a great San Diego tradition. The California grey whales pass close to shore each year as they migrate between Alaskan waters and the lagoons of Baja California. In the beginning, watchers gathered on Point Loma to view the whales from the land; the first picture shows the traffic jam on January 19, 1958. In

time, people began to go out on boats to see the mammoth mammals up close. The practice began in 1959 with Dr. Raymond Gilmore of Scripps Institution of Oceanography and the San Diego Natural History Museum. For decades he took four thousand visitors a year out for narrated trips. Such excursions have now become a

major wintertime industry, serving local citizens and tourists alike. On such a trip, the viewers get closeups, such as this whale going down just a few yards off the boat. Photographs courtesy of the Cabrillo National Monument and the San Diego Convention and Visitors Bureau

Yet another example of the scientific bent of this Sunbelt city is the Space Theatre, which opened in Balboa Park in 1973. It was named for Rueben H. Fleet, whose Consolidated Aircraft brought aerospace to San Diego in a large way in 1935. The theatre includes a projection system which can project ten thousand stars at any point of the sky at any point of history. It is also used for cinematic productions which surround the audience. The theatre, plus a science museum, is housed in a Spanish Colonial style building designed to continue the architectural tradition begun with the 1915 Panama California Exposition. Photograph courtesy of the San Diego Convention and Visitors Bureau

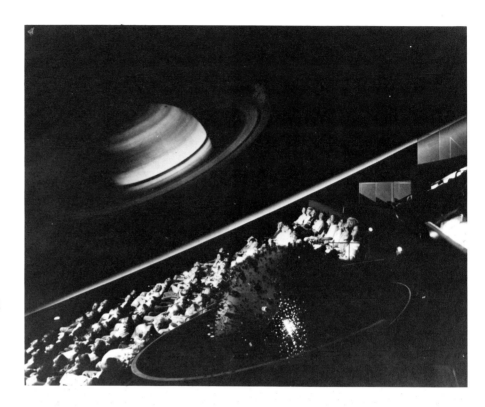

Balboa Park has remained the center of San Diego and the Zoo has remained the heart of Balboa Park. In 1952 Charles Schroeder replaced Belle Benchley as director of the San Diego Zoo, and took it to even greater heights. He pioneered medical research, professionalization of the operation, better business procedures, and expanded breeding programs. One of his most notable innovations was the Children's Zoo. When constructed in 1956-57, it was considered a new and radical idea. It included special exhibits of interest to children, and exhibits which mixed the visitor and zoo animals together in the same space. One example was the petting pen where visitors, like this young tourist from Texas, could (however cautiously) mingle with some of the animals. The Children's Zoo has been duplicated in zoos the worldover, and the successful practice of mixing visitor and visitee has been introduced to other parts of the San Diego Zoo. Photograph from the author's collection

Charles Schroeder's other innovation at the Zoo was the creation of the Wild Animal Park in San Pasqual Valley north of San Diego. It was originally conceived of as a site for expanded breeding of animals, especially endangered species. In time the San Diego Zoo became convinced the operation could serve an educational and entertainment function as well. Thus ground was broken in 1969 and in 1972 the Wild Animal Park opened its doors to visitors. The animals live in large areas, grouped by continent, and are viewed by visitors from a quiet monorail which encircles the area. There is also a visitor village with more exhibits and visitor services. The breeding operations have been extraordinarily successful and several species have been saved from extinction. One species has bred so well that specimens are now being reintroduced to its native habitat. This photograph shows the African area, where giraffes are sharing their habitat with rhinoceros, as they would in the wild. Photograph from the author's collection

In 1969 San Diego marked its two-hundreth anniversary with a relatively low key celebration. It lasted the whole year, with a variety of public events keyed to the July 16 anniversary of Father Junipero Serra's raising of the cross on Presidio Hill. One of the major byproducts of the bicentennial celebration was the creation of Old Town State Historical Park on the site of the first town. It was mostly the result of the work of state legislator James Mills (a former curator of the Serra Museum) and included acqusition of land and some remains of original buildings. A program of gradual restoration and reconstruction is planned to provide the area an appearance which interprets the original village. This 1969 poster tries to call attention to the Hispanic past of the new city of skyscrapers. Poster courtesy of the San Diego Historical Society Research Archives

SAN DIEGO
200th anniversary · 1969
a county-wide celebration

The theme of San Diego history since 1972 is "America's Finest City."
Nothing finer was seen in that period than the *Star of India* in full sail to
celebrate the United States Bicentennial on July 4, 1976. The *Star,*, flagship
of the San Diego Maritime Museum and an institution on the waterfront
since 1927, had not sailed under her own power for fifty-three years prior
to 1976. The historic sailing was viewed by thousands on land and sea; it
was the highlight of San Diego's celebration of two hundred years of
independence. Photograph courtesy of the Maritime Museum of San Diego

10

America's Finest City: San Diego Since 1972

—

In 1972 San Diego had been selected by President Richard Nixon as the site for the Republican National Convention. After a series of scandals, some with San Diego connections, the Republicans moved the convention to Miami. Some cities would have felt defeated by this, but as Neil Morgan poined out in his book prompted by the non-event, *San Diego: The Unconventional City*, failure is what has made San Diego great. For instance, its failure to get the railroad connections to the East prevented its becoming a smokestack-ridden factory town. It became instead a city of parks and flowers.

To counter bad publicity over the transfer of the convention, the dynamic young mayor, Pete Wilson, directed the creation of an America's Finest City Festival to celebrate San Diego's glories. The festival captured the imagination of the people and was continued for several years under the direction of Donna Damson, a member of Wilson's staff. More importantly, the concept became San Diego's self-selected, self-congratulatory tag for itself. *America's Finest City* began to appear in speeches, advertisements, and everyday conversation. Since 1972, it has been an appropriate label for San Diego.

The city is developing its downtown and beautifying its waterfront in a spectacular way. A sixteen block section of old Victorian buildings downtown has been revitalized since 1972 into the Gaslamp District. A Centre City Development Corporation has been created to direct an innovative combination of public and private funds into the revitalization of the inner city; including new highrises, often constructed with fountains, gardens and landscaping around them; a new transit system—the "Tijuana Trolley"; and landscaping along downtown city streets. The centerpiece of downtown redevelopment is Horton Plaza, an inner-city shopping area designed to capture the feeling of a Mediterranean seaport, with pastel colors, varying levels, plazas, street performers, and flags. It incorporates theatres and art galleries into its basically commercial base. The city is also encouraging the construction of downtown housing, to increase foot traffic and to support downtown theatres, galleries, restaurants, and stores. An artist colony is emerging in some old warehouses, and new hotels are being built to accommodate increasing numbers of visitors. The major building in a "new" downtown will be a "world class" convention center, to be built on the Embarcadero by the Unified Port District, and operated by the city. The physical, commercial and cultural development of downtown since the mid-1970s has created a sense of excitement and movement unequalled in many American cities of the period.

San Diego has other claims to being "America's Finest City." It is flowering culturally. The San Diego Opera is one of the most successful regional companies in the nation, attracting to the local stage the most distinguished singers in the world. The San Diego Symphony has improved musically and has rebuilt the Fox Theatre into a plush new Symphony Hall. If it can solve its financial problems, the San Diego Symphony can become an institution of national calibre. Few cities in the nation can match the theatre scene in San Diego. The Old Globe complex won a special Tony Award for distinction as a regional theatre in 1984. The La Jolla Playhouse, revived through the generosity of philanthropist Mandell Weiss, is acquiring a national reputation. One of its productions went from San Diego to Broadway and won most of the year's awards for best musical of the season. Downtown San Diego has several semi-professional and amateur drama groups, including one in Horton Plaza. There are thriving neighborhood theatre groups, children's theatre organizations, and university programs turning out performers who are achieving national reputations. The Balboa Park's Starlight Theatre performs traditional American musicals to full houses all summer long.

Another indication of San Diego's cultural maturity is the large number of museums it supports. Balboa Park contains museums of anthropology, photography, sports, Chicano culture, science, aerospace, and natural history and has a space theatre. Balboa Park is also home to the city's major art gallery, which is supplemented by La Jolla's art museum dedicated to contemporary art. San Diego also has one of two major maritime museums in the West, and San Diego's is unique in that its historic vessels actually sail!

Yet another indication of San Diego's growing distinction comes from its universities. The University of California branch in La Jolla has acquired almost instant glory for its scientific, medical, and technological research. The University's faculty ranks second only to Cal Tech in the ratio of National

SAN DIEGO

"America's Finest City" became San Diego's symbol after a disaster over the 1972 Republican National Convention. President Richard Nixon wanted the convention in San Diego, despite the lack of adequate facilities. The matter was complicated by a series of scandals unfolding in the Nixon administration and eventually the convention was transferred to Miami. It is said that city officials broke out bottles of champagne when the news was announced; one radio station celebrated by playing the theme "Exodus" over and over again. To replace the convention, San Diego's dynamic young mayor Pete Wilson organized an America's Finest City Festival. The festival continued for many years under the direction of Donna Damson, a member of Wilson's staff. The logo was used for years to convey the message of "America's Finest City." The community has picked up the theme and uses it frequently in advertisements and promotions, as well as in self-congratulation. Photograph from the author's collection

The thrust of San Diego politics in the 1970s was controlled growth and quality of life. A young legislator, Pete Wilson, rode that theme to the mayor's office and dominated local politics until elected to the United States Senate in 1982. The Wilson administration worked on controlling growth, on preserving open spaces and canyons, control of ugly billboards, and landscaping of public streets.

Obviously, many builders and developers opposed his administration and his programs; so, too, did many local labor unions, who saw controlled growth as an elitist program denying workers jobs and driving up the cost of living. This 1974 parade of union members on Broadway illustrates that sentiment. Photograph courtesy of the Center for Regional History, San Diego State University

The recognition of former hostage Richard Morefield (San Diego High School class of 1947) on January 31, 1981, marked the end of San Diego's ordeal in the Iranian Hostage Crisis. The crisis began in 1979 when Iranian rebels seized fifty-three hostages in Tehran and ended in January 1981. Dorothy Morefield, Richard's wife, was a spokesperson for the families of the hostages throughout the crisis. She was accessible, articulate and effective. Although her bluntness and criticism of the State Department offended some, Dorothy Morefield was heroic in her own right. Thus the ceremony of welcome which began on January 28, 1981, with a motorcade from the airport to the Morefield home and ended with a ceremony in Balboa Park featuring the mayor, the governor, and other dignitaries, was as much for her as for her husband. Photograph courtesy of Jerry Hebert

Academy of Science winners to its faculty (one to ten, in fact). San Diego State University has become one of the nation's largest urban universities. A poll by *California Higher Education* ranked it first among the California State University system's nineteen institutions, and twice the *U.S. News and World Report* has ranked it as one of the nation's best comprehensive universities. Many departments and programs are accredited; for instance its Graduate School of Public Health is one of only twenty-three accredited institutions in the United States. In general, education is a key factor in the nature of San Diego since 1972, shaping the nature of its economy and the quality of its life. In the 1980s, the level of education of the community as a whole is the highest of any major metropolitan area in the United States.

When the above is coupled with the unexcelled climate, the physical beauty of the setting, and the almost unlimited recreational facilities, San Diego has a sound basis for claiming to be a good place to live. Apparently many people agree, because population has continued to grow rapidly. It passed 1,000,000 in 1986 and San Diego is now the seventh largest city in the country. The population of the metropolitan area exceeds 2,300,000. The growth has been made possible by a continued military presence (it still accounts for almost one-fifth of the local economy), plus growth in manufacturing, service industries, and the visitor industries. The economy is becoming increasingly more diversified.

There are many reasons why San Diego could call itself the nation's finest city. That does not mean that there are not some severe problems which have emerged in San Diego since 1972, and which threaten its future.

Probably the largest problem is growth. As San Diego continues to grow, problems of flooding, water sources, aesthetics, pollution, traffic control, and the general quality of life become more and more severe. The area is inundated with construction, which is increasingly destroying what makes San Diego unique, and which is making San Diego more and more like the colossus to the north. Not only is growth destroying the quality of life, but it often destroys some of the historic and aesthetic landmarks with it. Major buildings of historic interest have been levelled to make way for a new subdivision or office building. As a group of concerned citizens found out when it tried to fight the Roman Catholic church's plan to build an all-purpose hall on top of parts of the major ruins of California's and Junipero Serra's first mission, Mission San Diego de Alcala, the developer-oriented preservation ordinance is very weak and provides no real protection of historic sites. If it is to preserve its unique heritage and quality of life, San Diego must develop ways of respecting its natural and its historic environment as it grows.

The city also has to face the realities of life as a sister city of Tijuana, Mexico. Tijuana has become a huge city with major problems of pollution, sewage disposal, crime—many of which spill over (in the case of sewage, literally) into San Diego. Although it tends to ignore its relationship with Tijuana, San Diego is inexorably tied to that city. Tijuana shoppers pour money into San Diego's economy, and Tijuana workers provide much of the labor for San Diego. In addition, plants over the border—called *Maquiladoras*—are an important element in San Diego's manufacturing industries. As the Hispanic population in San Diego grows, and it is expected to account for one-fourth of the population by 1990, the cultural ties will also become closer. Thus San Diego must begin to work with and integrate Tijuana into its planning and growth.

San Diego also needs to recognize and integrate into the power structure its other racial and ethnic minorities. San Diego is becoming less and less an Anglo City, yet there is little evidence of this in the power structure. The failure to

San Diego may be "America's Finest City," but that does not mean that there are no problems in paradise. Two frequent ones are fire and water. The fires usually occur in summer and fall when "Santa Ana" conditions bring high winds, heat, and low humidity. An extremely disastrous fire occurred on June 30, 1985, when sixty-four homes and eighteen other buildings were destroyed in Normal Heights. The floods occur on the relatively rare occasions when it rains. The city has seen massive floods in the 1860s, 1884, 1916, and 1927, but dams in the Backcountry have limited the flood damage con-siderably. Heavy rains still, however, create floods and mudslides, such as the flooding of the San Diego River in Mission Valley in 1980. The river floor has been developed since 1959 when the City Council authorized Mission Valley Shopping Center over the objections of city staff who pointed out the potential for flooding. In the quarter century since that deci-sion, almost the entire valley floor has been developed, but nothing has been done to deal with the flood problem. Photograph courtesy of the San Diego Historical Society—Ticor Collection

encourage minority *entré* into the power structure and the society as a whole has led to alienation of many minorities and to the growth of such problems as hostility to the police and youth gangs (almost always formed on a racial or ethnic basis). Ways to recognize and utilize its non-white, non-WASP peoples must be found if San Diego is to avoid being split into permament enclaves of hostile populations.

The city must also grow up, and outgrow a transient-get-rich-quick mentality. San Diego today is a young city with many attracted to the area for the opportunities it offers. The result has been a high level of corruption, as exemplified in the 1970s by the C. Arnold Smith financial empire's collapse, and in the 1980s by the J. David Dominelli ponzi scheme, which drew many down with it. This attitude has been shown in politics as development and growth-oriented policies have usually dominated. It has also shown itself in political corruption. When Pete Wilson was elected mayor in 1971, one reason why his predecessor was turned out was a taxicab scandal. Wilson's successor had to resign after being convicted of felony violations of the election campaign code. A few years earlier a city councilman was removed after conviction of a felony and currently another is under indictment. The city desperately needs to develop leadership which looks beyond the "bottom line" and into the future and the kind of city we will be leaving to the next generation.

If San Diego faces and resolves all of its challenges, it can become the model for American cities of the future, and it can hold on to its claim as being "America's Finest City." If it cannot deal with the challenges of the future, the 1980s will probably be known as the "Golden Age" of San Diego and it will plunge into a Los Angeles-like torpor of congestion, ugliness, pollution, and racial and ethnic unrest and violence.

Regardless of its future, it is clear that San Diego has come a long way since Junipero Serra and the motley band of Spanish soldiers and priests established the first European settlement here in 1769. Even its modern founder, Alonzo Horton, would probably be surprised to see what he hath wrought. *San Diego: A Pictorial History* has traced that growth of San Diego from a miserable little place on the edge of the earth into America's seventh largest city, and perhaps its finest. Armed with a better knowledge of its past, the community can now better direct its future!

The opening of the James S. Copley Library in La Jolla is another example of San Diego's recent maturing as a cultural center. The Library is a memorial to James S. Copley, whose Copley Press has owned the *San Diego Union* and *Tribune* since 1928. The library is housed in an elegant building dedicated in 1982, and includes an art collection, artifacts, books, and manuscripts. It is strong in western materials (especially on Mark Twain), and in manuscripts from the American Revolution, including letters of most of the signers of the Declaration of Independence. The library is small and specialized and brings to the city a collection of items beyond the utilitarian materials which local public libraries and universities could afford. This view of the main salon shows the Peter Hurd portrait of James S. Copley at the far end of the room. Photograph courtesy of the James C. Copley Library

In recent years San Diego has played a major role in the America's Cup twelve-meter yacht challenge. A San Diegan, Gerald Driscoll, revolutionized the process of entry in 1974 when he created a syndicate using tax-free donations. That pattern began to be followed by others, thus breaking the hold of wealthy easterners on the race. Another San Diegan, Dennis Conner, created such a syndicate in 1980 which successfully defended the cup in the vessel *Freedom*. Unfortunately, in 1983 Conner became the first American since the Cup was created in 1851 to lose it to a foreigner. He and his crew outsailed the Australian challenger, but he could not overcome the technical superiority of *Australia II*. Undaunted, Conner and his syndicate have raised $12 million to outfit three vessels in order to try to recapture the America's Cup in Perth in 1987. This photograph shows the *Freedom* and *Enterprise* in a practice race on March 16, 1980, with the *Star of India* and the San Diego skyline in the background. Photograph courtesy of the Maritime Museum of San Diego

A major cultural success story has been the San Diego Opera, whose 1986 production of *Otello*, with Giuseppi Giacomini as Otello and Silvano Curroli as Iago, is shown here. The Company has acquired national distinction and attracts major stars. It is both an artistic and financial success, probably at least partially because of the widespread network of opera supporters it has organized throughout the region. The San Diego Symphony, by contrast, has had a more mixed existence. Under the direction of Conductor David Atherton, it has achieved musical distinction. The Symphony boldly purchased an old movie theatre, the Fox, which it spent milions remodeling into a symphony hall. Unfortunately, the symphony's financial situation has been precarious as it has been buffeted by one fiscal crisis after another. Photograph courtesy of the San Diego Opera

While the power structure of San Diego has been dominated by Anglo-Americans since shortly after the American take-over in 1846, many other cultures have and still live in the city. The 1980 census, for instance, identified thirty-one ethnic and racial groups in the city. Many groups merge into the economic mainstream of the city, but still find ways to maintain their own identity and culture. An example is the Indian Pow Wow. Several are held each year in the area, and they give Indians a chance to come together to share and celebrate their cultures. These dancers are at San Diego State University, whose annual Pow Wow every spring is one of the largest in the county. Photograph courtesy of the San Diego State University Department of American Indian Studies

The largest ethnic minority in San Diego is the Hispanic community, which formed 14.8 percent of the area's population in the 1980 census. This represented a 127 percent increase over 1970 and it is projected that by the 1990 census, the Spanish-speaking population will reach 25 percent of the total population. Since the 1970s, there has been some recognition of Hispanic culture in the city, including the creation of the Centro Cultural de la Raza in Balboa Park. In October 1981, a new mural was dedicated in the Centro Cultural. The honored guest was Jose Gonzales (waving to the audience) who had ridden with Pancho Villa in the Mexican Revolution. The Chicano muralist Victor Ochoa is on the far right. Photograph courtesy of Jerry Hebert

Although San Diego since 1972 has developed an exciting new downtown, a larger visitor industry, more diversified service and manufacturing industries, it is still very much a "Navy Town." In 1986 San Diego had the largest concentration of Naval power in the free world, with 110,000 uniformed personnel, or about 20 percent of the United States Navy stationed here. To put it another way, 19 percent of the 1985 gross regional product of San Diego County came from the military. Every weekend the Navy provides a reminder of its presence in the community by docking a vessel on Broadway Pier for the public to visit. Photograph courtesy of the San Diego Convention and Visitors Bureau

In recent years Southeast Asians have moved to San Diego in large numbers. They include people evacuated by the Americans before the fall of Saigon and boat people and refugees who have fled since then. A 1983-84 study indicates that there were about sixty thousand Indochinese in San Diego at that point, and about half of them were Vietnamese. About 40 percent lived in Linda Vista, another 40 percent in East San Diego, 14 percent in North Park and the rest scattered throughout the city. They have quickly adapted to their new world and in the last five years unemployment has dropped from 42 percent to 15 percent; welfare dependency from 44 percent to 11 percent and average family income has doubled to $22,600. Southeast Asians are working in factories, service industries, and in their own small business such as this restaurant in East San Diego. As illustrated by the picture of the three generations of a family at a 1982 Tet Celebration, the family unit is strong among the Southeast Asians and has provided a base for their successful assimilation. Photographs courtesy of Ray T. Smith

The clown lying in the street is not crazy; he is part of the publicity to prepare San Diego for its new trolley, which began service on July 26, 1981. As San Diego tackled problems of pollution and congestion, it turned to a new mass transit system. Utilizing some of the lines of the old San Diego and Arizona Railroad system, the Metropolitan Transit Board built a 15.9-mile trolley system from the Santa Fe depot, through the center of the city, and down to the Mexican border. It was built under budget, on time, and with a daily ridership of nearly twenty-thousand, its fares cover most of its operating cost. It was quickly dubbed the "Tijuana Trolley" (to the consternation of some local officials) and attracted

world wide attention for its economic success. The operation is being expanded eastward, and plans include further expansion to the airport and other parts of the region. Photograph courtesy of Jerry Hebert

If Alonzo Horton could come back to San Diego today, he would be surprised, if not shocked, to see what has happened across the street from his old Horton House. He would find a downtown of skyscrapers and a huge, colorful shopping area where he had found chaparral and nothing else in 1869. He would find that the centerpiece of that downtown was named after him—Horton Plaza—and that it was the core of a major revitalization of the downtown of what has become the United States' seventh largest city. As a developer/builder/salesman/promoter of the first order, Alonzo Horton would probably be very pleased!

The man who built Horton Plaza is Ernest W. Hahn. In most cities, if you wanted to show the people who most shaped the place, you would show mayors or legislators or philanthropists. In San Diego, you must show a builder and developer; it has been that way since Alonzo Horton arrived in 1869. In this case, the builder/developer is Ernest Hahn, who began a contracting firm in 1946. By 1983 his firm had built thirty-nine major regional shopping centers and been involved in eleven redevelopment projects. In San Diego, he had helped the earlier decline of downtown by building such regional shopping centers as Fashion Valley and University Towne Center. In 1974 he was selected by the Centre City Development Corporation to plan and implement the redevelopment of San Diego's core with the Horton Plaza project. He is shown on October 18, 1983, driving a bulldozer down Third Avenue on his way to the groundbreaking for that development. Photograph courtesy of Jerry Herbert

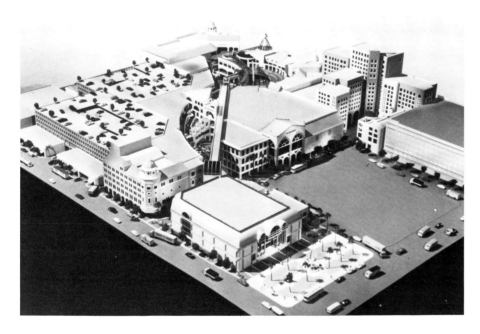

This model shows the overall scope of the Horton Plaza Project. It covers 11.5 acres and 6.5 city blocks in the very heart of downtown San Diego. The first phase includes 900,000 square feet of leasable area (and a second phase will add another 300,000 square feet). The city spent about $33,000,000 to assemble and prepare the site, and private funds contributed over $140,000,000 to build the Plaza. It will be anchored by four major department stores and will include 190 other retail establishments and a 2,800-car parking structure. The project opened in August 1985 after a decade of incredibly complex fits and starts. Horton Plaza represents a new way to combine public and private funds for downtown development; it is important enough that the MIT Center for Real Estate Development has published a two-volume study, *Horton Plaza, San Diego: A Case Study of Public-Private Development* (1985) which is the best source of information on those detailed and complex processes whereby it came into being. Photograph courtesy of the San Diego Convention and Visitors Bureau

This photograph by Beverly Schroeder shows the unique design of Horton Plaza. The idea was to create an old-world festival atmosphere such as might be found in a Mediterranean seaport town. The design features multiple levels, narrow passages, curves and corners, fountains, courtyards, many color schemes, and considerable use of art. With flags flying, colorful peddler carts, street performers, and the frequent good smells of delicious food, Horton Plaza is designed to entice a suburban automobile-oriented community back downtown. Photograph courtesy of the Centre City Development Corporation

This spectacular photograph by Ken Jacques of the entrance to Horton Plaza tells several stories. One story is the obelisk in the center. It has already become a much reproduced symbol of San Diego and downtown. The obelisk is one of three pieces of art commissioned especially for Horton Plaza and was done by San Francisco artist and professor Joan Brown. The other story in the picture is the word *Lyceum* in the lower foreground. It represents an $8,300,000 theatre complex to be operated by San Diego Repertory Theatre. This inclusion of two theatres in a shopping mall was done partially to replace the 1913 Lyceum Theatre which was demolished to make space for the parking garage. It was also done to create a total downtown atmosphere—culture, restaurants, shopping, offices, and even homes—which would bring foot traffic back to the center of the city. It is a unique blending of culture and commerce which is one of the characteristics of the whole downtown revitalization project which makes San Diego "America's Finest City" in the mid-1980s. Photograph courtesy of Ken Jacques

A major part of downtown reinvigoration is the Gaslamp Quarter. This is a preservation district covering over sixteen blocks and focusing on Fifth Avenue south of Broadway. That was the main street of San Diego in Alonzo Horton's day and is still filled with Victorian structures which were left behind when the focus of San Diego's downtown shifted to Broadway after 1900. In 1974 a district was created to foster economic revitalization and to preserve the unique historical architecture of the area. It was designed to stress pedestrian uses and to complement the Horton Plaza redevelopment, which would be adjacent. Gradually the buildings have been refurbished to their original glory, as seen in the first picture. The neighborhood has been redone with brick paving, gaslamp-style street lights and landscaping. The other photograph shows Mayor Pete Wilson addressing the audience at the dedication of the brick paving. To his left is "Alonzo Horton." Most of the redevelopment of downtown San Diego was begun during Wilson's administration, 1971-1983. Photographs courtesy of San Diego Convention and Visitors Bureau, and Jerry Hebert

With the arrival of *Azure Seas* in January 1983, San Diego saw the return of cruise ships to the harbor. The city had worked hard to make that happen, including the investment of $3,700,000 in remodeling of the old "B" Street Pier into a modern tour ship terminal and parking facility. Ships such as the one pictured here, Princess Cruise's *Pacific Princess*, the "Love Boat" of television fame, have begun to call in San Diego as part of cruises to the Mexican Riviera and elsewhere. The development of the cruise ship industry and the plans to develop a major convention center on the waterfront (to be built by the Unified Port District and to be run by the city) are all part of the effort to capitalize on the visitor industry. In 1985 tourism brought twenty-nine million visitors to San Diego, created eighty-three thousand jobs and poured over $2,000,000,000 into the economy. Photograph courtesy of the San Diego Convention and Visitors Bureau

On January 18, 1986, Old Town State Park moved closer to the recreation of the Old Town during the 1821-1872 period when it dedicated three more reconstructions on the old plaza. The three new buildings were the U.S. House, the Light-Freeman House, and the Casa de Wrightington. In the photograph Acting Mayor Ed Struiksma is speaking to the dedication gathering in front of the U.S. House. The building was reconstructed as it would have looked in the 1850s. The original was one of the prefabricated buildings shipped to San Diego from New England. This showed the determination of the Americans to impose their culture and way of life on the newly conquered city, whether that culture made environmental sense or not. The other two buildings dedicated the same day were of adobe/tile

construction in the Hispanic tradition. They represented a much better utilization of available materials than the Yankee wooden buildings which had to be imported from thousands of miles away. Photograph courtesy of Old Town State Park

San Diego is blessed with many Victorian buildings erected during the boom years of the 1880s. As the city has grown, many have been threatened with destruction. In 1969 a concerned group of citizens formed Save Our Heritage Organization (SOHO) to preserve Victorian architecture in San Diego; since then they have broadened their scope to cover all aspects of San Diego's architectural heritage. Their initial efforts led San Diego County to create Heritage Park, where endangered Victorian structures could be relocated and preserved. The first photograph shows the Bushyhead House being moved in 1976 from its 232 Cedar Street location to Heritage Park. It had been built in 1887 by Edward Bushyhead, an early sheriff and owner of a newspaper. The second photograph shows the relocated house after being refurbished in Heritage Park. Other buildings in view are (left to right) the Burton House (1893 Classic Revival-Late Victorian); the Sherman Gilbert House (an 1882 Eastlake structure with widow's walk); the Bushyhead House; and, behind the tree, the Queen Anne style Christian House (1889). While these houses have been preserved, San Diego has lost other buildings and sites because of lack of community concern or because of weak preservation legislation. For instance the Klauber House, a prime example of the work of San Diego's most important architect, Irving Gill, was destroyed several years ago; the site is still a vacant lot. The Roman Catholic diocese is pursuing plans to build a multipurpose building atop major ruins of the California's first mission, Mission San Diego de Alcala. In "America's Finest City," sometimes preservation of the past takes a back seat to growth of the present. Photographs courtesy of the Save Our Heritage Organization

In the 1980s Balboa Park is still the source of immense pride among San Diegans. As this 1980 photograph shows, it can be a very busy place on a weekend afternoon. The old exposition areas are still graced by many of the Spanish baroque buildings of the 1915 Panama California Exposition, complemented by lush landscaping. The large number of attractions in the park include several art galleries, an artists' colony, a model railroad, a space theatre, and museums of photography, sports, Chicano culture, science, aerospace, and natural history. The San Diego Historical Society Archives, the House of Pacific Relations, and the San Diego Zoo are all located in the park. Although much of the use of the park is by local citizens, a 1983 study showed that it drew over four million tourists each year, creating about five thousand jobs for the city. Photograph from the author's collection

Are your lions bored? These San Diego Zoo lions certainly seemed so on June 5, 1980, when they were photographed. If so, what to do about it? One thing is to reorganize your zoo to eliminate individual exhibits and to combine plants and animals into bio-climatic exhibits. That is what the San Diego Zoo plans to as it approaches its seventy-fifth anniversary (1991). The concept involves development of exhibits of plants and animals who live in a common bio-climatic zone, such as rain forests, savannas, islands, or deserts. That will provide the plants and animals a more natural setting, and give the human visitor a better understanding of the natural world. An example would be a savanna grasslands environment, which would include elephants, rhinoceros, crowned cranes, a giant anteater, a giraffe, zebras, spotted hyenas and a patas monkey. The first of such bio-climatic exhibits at the San Diego Zoo will be in the Cascade Canyon area, where a rain forest climate will be created. Photograph from the author's collection

One feature of the 1935 California Pacific International Exposition in Balboa Park was a replica of Shakespeare's Old Globe Theatre. It was meant to be demolished after the Exposition, but it was not, and survived to be the oldest professional theatre in California and the American theatre with the longest continuing commitment to the production of Shakespeare's plays. In time the Old Globe was supplemented by a theatre "in-the-round" and, when the Old Globe burned in 1978, an outdoor stage, the Festival Stage. The burned theatre was rebuilt and opened in 1982, as photographed by Ken Howard at that time. Under the leadership of Craig Noel and, more recently, Jack O'Brien, the Old Globe has acquired national distinction as a major regional theatre, and was awarded a Special Tony Award for outstanding achievement in 1984. Today the Old Globe presents a mixture of Shakespeare and other drama, draws some exciting actors to supplement its own staff, and regularly sells in excess of 90 percent of all seats by subscription. The Old Globe is another reason why San Diego can make claim to being "America's Finest City." Photograph courtesy of the Old Globe

The highlight of San Diego's sports history came on September 21, 1984, when the San Diego Padres beat the Chicago Cubs to win the National League Championship. That victory came after fifteen years of struggle as an expansion team; a struggle which began to turn around only after hamburger tycoon Ray Kroc bought the team and provided adequate support. In the championship series, San Diego spotted Chicago a two-game lead before coming back to win it all. The "Oh Doctor" headline refers to San Diego sportscaster Jerry Coleman's excited comments when Steve Garvey hit a homer to win the final game. In the World Series, Padre No. 7, Kurt Bevacqua hit a dramatic homer for a 5-3 victory in game two, but San Diego lost the Series to the

Detroit Tigers in five games. Photographs courtesy of the San Diego Padres

Abundant recreational possibilities help make San Diego an attractive city. In addition to the usual activities—beaches, fishing, water skiing, sail boarding, surfing, yachting, golf, tennis, walking, running, and many more—San Diego offers some unusual attractions to tempt the doer and the watcher. One is hang gliding. Although it is done at several San Diego area locations, probably the most popular is the Torrey Pines Cliffs, where hang gliding shares a facility with gliders. This hang glider is taking off before the usual weekend crowd of spectators. La Jolla is in the background. Photograph courtesy of the San Diego Convention and Visitors Bureau

Another San Diego recreational activity is skin diving. One of the most popular spots is an aquatic park off the La Jolla Cove. It is regarded by divers as one of the most beautiful diving sites between the Virgin Islands and Hawaii. This photograph also shows swimmers and beach lovers at the Cove. Scripps Institution of Oceanography and its research pier are in the distance, with the University of California's San Diego campus in the far background. Photograph courtesy of the San Diego Convention and Visitors Bureau

Over-the-line is a San Diego beach adaptation of baseball for three persons. It has become a local institution which is played throughout the year by old and young, beautiful and homely. It comes into its own each summer with the Over-the-Line World Championship Tournament put on since 1954 by the Old Mission Beach Athletic Club (OMBAC). Begun with eight teams, it now draws nearly nine hundred entries and crowds of over twenty thousand who come to watch the games, the nearly-naked spectators and players, and to drink heavily. A major feature of the tournament is the selection of Miss Emerson, usually the most buxom woman in the smallest bikini. Another favored part of the competition is the names chosen for the teams; most are too obscene to be repeated in mixed company. Indeed, national television companies have frequently investigated the possibilities of televising the proceedings, but each time the proposals have fallen through because OMBAC refused to require the cleaning up of the team names. Thus OTL remains a distinctly and privately San Diego function— one that does much to define what makes "American's Finest City" unique. Photograph courtesy of the San Diego Convention and Visitors Bureau

The skyline of San Diego in 1984
shows how far it has come from the
1840s, when it was called a miserable
place on the edge of the earth. By the
mid-1980s San Diego's population had
officially exceeded one million people
and it was the seventh largest city in
the nation. In addition, San Diego
had begun to develop a spectacular
new downtown-Embarcadero area.
Its growth was fueled by an ever-
diversifying economy, albeit one with
a still heavy emphasis on the military
and tourism. With its superb climate,
the large number of recreational
opportunities, and with the flowering
of its cultural institutions, San Diego
may well be "America's Finest City."
Photograph courtesy of the San
Diego Convention and Visitors
Bureau

Bibliographical Essay

It is impossible to prepare a book like *San Diego: A Pictorial History* without drawing upon the work of hundreds of scholars who have been there before you. To list each individual item consulted for this book would take more space than the book itself. It is only possible to acknowledge generally the contribution of others, and to describe the major types of sources and list the names of some of the authors whose work was most frequently used.

Much information was obtained at the Research Archives of the San Diego Historical Society. The most heavily used items were the vertical files, the biography files, manuscript collections, unpublished manuscripts of books, articles and reports, ephemera, as well as books, pamphlets and other items often not available elsewhere. The Society's oral history program was indispensible; much life was brought to the book from the interviews with Horace Allen, De Graff Austin, Sam Hamill, Alice Heyneman, Bob Johnson, Katherine Leng, Elizabeth MacPhail, Burnham Marston, Ivan Messenger, Marie Mayrhofer, Glenn Rick, Jeanne Rimmer, George Ruhlen, Katherine Taylor, Isabel Tinkham, and Mandell Weiss. Similar types of material were consulted at the San Diego State University Center for Regional History.

Masters theses and doctoral dissertations were another important source of material on San Diego. Most of those used were from San Diego State University and were by Thurman Austin, Dana Basney, Alice Blankfort, Robert Carlton, Thomas Carnes, Marilyn Clark, Edward Clarkson, Mary Flaherty, Andrew Griego, Judith Liu, Rebecca Lytle, Paul Lucas, Mary Miller, Herbert Nelson, Uldis Ports, Gerald Schlenker, Charlotte Villalobos, William Richardson, and Maurice Tompkins. Theses and dissertations used from other institutions were by Roy Harris, Richard Carrico, Susan Carrico, Grace Miller and Patricia Kenner.

San Diego: A Pictorial History simply could not have been done without the source materials and articles published since the 1950s in the *Journal of San Diego History*. The authors and editors of items consulted include Lynn Adkins; Richard Amero; Robert Archibald; Jane Booth; Larry Booth; John Brownlee; Robert Carlton; Richard Carrico; Thomas Case; Trudie Casper; Pliny Castanien; Adelaida Castillo; Clare Crane; Kathleen Crawford; Harry W. Crosby; Ben F. Dixon; Lucille DuVall; Lucinda Eddy; Iris Engstrand; Donald Estes; William E. Evans; Paul Ezell; Helen Ferris; Robert Fikes, Jr.; Robert Frazer; Mario T. Garcia, Clifford Graves; Andrew Griego; Richard Griswold del Castillo; Edgar Hebert; Robert F. Heilbron; Robert Heizer; Ruth Held; Gregg Hennessey; Charles Hughes; A. E. Jansen; Sally Johns; Bruce Kamerling; Ann Kantor; Lucy Killea; James E. Kirby; Marilyn Kneeland; C. D. Kroll; Gary F. Kurutz; Blaine P. Lamb; Lawrence Lee; Diana Lindsay; Zelma Locker; Douglas Lowell; and Rebecca Lytle. Also Elizabeth MacPhail, Gail Madyun, Larry Malone, W. Michael Mathes, Ronald V. May, Arthur F. McEvoy, James Mills, Beth Mohr, Gregory Montes, James R. Moriarty, James E. Moss, Richard Muller, Abraham P. Nasatir, Norman Neuerburg, Frank Norris, Broeck Oder, Thomas Patterson, Martin Peterson, Nicholas C. Polos, Beverly Potter, Uldis Ports, Ronald Quinn, George Ruhlen, Patricia Schaelchlin, Thomas Scharf, Gerald Schlenker, Henry Schwartz, Margaret A. Secor, Manuel P. Servin, Rosalie Shanks, Marjorie Shaw, Elizabeth Shor, Harold P. Simonson, Jean Smith, Michael Stepner, Norton B. Stern; Jefferson K. Stickney, Mary Taschner, Sally Thorton, William Uberti, Stephen Van Wormer, Ralph H. Vigil, Davis Weber, Martha M. White, Richard B. Yale, John F. Yurtinus, and Orion Zink. Other articles were used in the *Western States Jewish Historical Quarterly, Western Historical Quarterly, Southern California Quarterly, California History,* and the *Pacific Historian.*

The *Brand Books* of the San Diego Corral of the Westerners had a lot of useful articles, as did many of the seminar papers published by the Cabrillo Historical Association: *Boat and Shipbuilding in San Diego* (1983), *The Cabrillo Era* (1982), *Fort Guijarros (1982), They Came from the Sea: A Maritime History of San Diego* (1979), and *The Military on Point Loma* (1985).

In preparing the book, it has been necessary on many topics to use newspapers and magazines for information. The most extensively used newspapers were the *Reader,* the *San Diego Union,* and the *Tribune*; the San Diego County edition of the *Los Angeles Times* was used less often. Of magazines, by far the most important was the *San Diego Magazine,* which has a long tradition of publishing historical articles. A number of people and institutions shared reports, documents and other materials: the San Diego Zoo, the Save Our Heritage Organization, the Klauber Wangenheim Company, and the Old Town State Park for example. The newsletters and publications of the San Diego Natural History Museum, the San Diego Zoo, the Museum of Man, the San Diego Aerospace Museum, and the San Diego Maritime Museum also were helpful. In addition, many scholars generously shared unpublished materials, including Stephen Van Wormer, Ronald V. May, Richard Carrico, Meredith Vezina, Judith Schille, Susan Lehman, and Cindy Malinick.

Obviously, books were important, too. Anyone writing on San Diego history has to use Richard Pourade, *History of San Diego* (7 vols., 1960-1977). Older general histories, such as William Smythe, *History of San Diego* (1908); and Clarence A. McGrew, *City of San Diego and County of San Diego* (2 vols., 1922) are helpful, if used cautiously. Other broad histories used were James Mills, *San Diego: Where California Began* (1976); Elizabeth MacPhail, *The Story of New San Diego and of its Founder Alonzo H. Horton* (2nd ed., 1979); Iris Engstrand, *San Diego: California's Cornerstone* (1980); Jerry MacMullen, *They Came by Sea* (1969); Neil Morgan and Tom Blair, *Yesterday's San Diego* (1976); Neil Morgan, *San Diego: The Unconventional City* (1972); and Syd Love, *San Diego: Portrait of a Spectacular City* (1969). An extremely useful handbook was Philip Pryde, editor, *San Diego: An Introduction to the Region* (2nd ed., 1984).

Some of the more important biographical or autobiographical items consulted were: Harry M. Wegeforth and Neil Morgan, *It Began with a Roar* (1953); Victoria Jacobs, *Diary of a San Diego Girl, 1856* (1974), edited by Sylvia Arden; William Wagner, *Reuben Fleet and the Story of Consolidated Aircraft* (1976); Ed Fletcher, *Memoirs* (1941);

H. Austin Adams, *The Man John D. Spreckels* (1924); Elizabeth MacPhail, *Kate Sessions* (1976); Lawrence Oliver, *Never Backward: The Autobiography of Lawrence Oliver, A Portuguese American* (1972); Oscar Cotton, *The Good Old Days* (1962), Mary Gilman Marston, compiler, *George White Marston* (2 vols, 1956); Belle J. Benchley, *My Life in a Man Made Jungle* (1940); Elizabeth Banning, *Helen Hunt Jackson* (1973); Andrew Rolle, *An American in California* (1956), Don Stewart, *Frontier Fort: A Chapter in San Diego's History* (1965), and Emma Goldman, *Living My Life* (1931).

Some more specialized books on early topics which were consulted in preparation of this book were: John Schutz, *Spain's Colonial Outpost* (1985); Francis Weber, editor, *The Proto Mission: A Documentary History of San Diego de Alcala* (n.d.), and *Some Reminiscences about Fray Junipero Serra* (1985); Edith Webb, *Indian Life at the Old Mission* (1952); Richard Carrico, *Stranger in a Stolen Land: American Indians in San Diego 1850-1880* (1986); George H. Phillips, *Chiefs and Challengers, Indian Resistance and Cooperation in Southern California* (1975); Lora Cline, *Just Before Sunset* (rev. ed., 1984); Richard Henry Dana, *Two Years Before the Mast* (1840); R. W. Brackett, *A History of the Ranchos* (1939); Cecil Moyer, *Historic Ranchos of San Diego* (1969); Ed Scott, *San Diego County Soldier-Pioneers, 1846-1866* (1976); Nellie V. Sanchez, *Spanish Arcadia* (1929); Joe Mora, *Californios* (1940); W. H. Emory, *Report on the United States and Mexican Survey* (1857); Henry Miller, *Account of a Tour of the California Mission & Town, 1856* (1985); Stephen A. Colston, ed., *Approaches to Historical Archaeology: The Case of the Royal Presidio of San Diego* (1982); Henry F. Dobyns, editor, *Spanish Colonial Frontier Research* (1980); and Ross Holland, *The Old Point Loma Lighthouse* (1968).

On the last century of San Diego history, specialized books used in preparing *San Diego: A Pictorial History* were: Helen Ellsberg, *Mines of Julian* (1972); Glenn Dumke, *The Boom of the Eighties in Southern California* (1944); Emmett Greenwalt, *California Utopia, Point Loma 1897-1942* (rev. ed., 1975); Patricia Schaelchlin, *The Little Clubhouse on Steamship Wharf* (1984); Edward Davis, *The U.S. Navy and U.S. Marine Corps in San Diego* (1955); Elretta Sudsbury, *Jackrabbits to Jets* (1967); Richard V. Dodge, *Rails of the Silver Gate: The Spreckels of San Diego Empire* (1960); Robert Hanft, *San Diego and Arizona: The Impossible Railroad* (1984); Clara Breed, *Turning the Pages: San Diego Public Library History, 1882-1982* (1983); Walter Swanson, *The Thin Gold Watch: A Personal History of the Newspaper Copleys* (1970); Florence Christman, *The Romance of Balboa Park* (rev. ed., 1985); Bill Bruns, *A World of Animals: The San Diego Zoo and Wild Animal Park* (1983); *Wild in the City: The Best of Zoonooz* (1985); Richard Reilly, *A Promise Kept: The Story of the James S. Copley Library* (1983); William J. McGill, *The Year of the Monkey: Revolt on Campus 1968-1969* (1982); Donald C. Bauder, *Captain Money and the Golden Girl: The J. David Affair* (1985); Gerald G. Kuhn and Francis Shepard, *Sea Cliffs, Beaches, and Costal Valleys of San Diego County* (1984); Karen Johl, *Timeless Treasures: San Diego's Victorian Heritage* (1982); Neil Morgan, *Westward Tilt: The American West Today* (1963); Neal R. Peirce, *The Pacific States of America: People, Politics and Power in the Five Pacific Basin States* (1972); Richard Bernard and Bradley Rice, editors, *Sunbelt Cities: Politics and Growth Since World War II* (1983); and Jacques Gordon, *Horton Plaza, San Diego: A Case Study of Public-Private Development* (2 vols., 1985).

Index